KNOWING THE
LAW IN
SPAIN

More related titles

Buy to Let in Spain
How to invest in Spanish property for pleasure and profit

'Any book that shows how to have a sun-kissed retirement and get someone else to pay for your holidays in Spain…has got to be worth getting hold of.' – Living Spain

Buying a Property in Spain
An insider guide to finding a home in the sun

'Whether it's renovating a ruin, renting a cosy cottage, or building your own home, this book will tell you exactly how to do it.' – Daily Mirror

Going to Live in Spain
A practical guide to enjoying a new lifestyle in the sun

'Tips on how to get the most out of this vibrant country so that you can enjoy your new life to the full.' – Sunday Telegraph

Gone to Spain
You too can realise your dream of a better lifestyle

'The author writes with honesty and directness. It is difficult not to be enthused by this book.' – Living Spain

howtobooks
Send for a free copy of the latest catalogue to:
How To Books
3 Newtec Place, Magdalen Road,
Oxford OX4 1RE, United Kingdom
email: info@howtobooks.co.uk
http://www.howtobooks.co.uk

KNOWING THE
LAW IN
SPAIN

A GUIDE TO SPANISH LAW FOR THE
BRITISH PROPERTY OWNER, RESIDENT
OR LONG-TERM VISITOR

HARRY KING

howtobooks

Published by How To Books Ltd,
3 Newtec Place, Magdalen Road,
Oxford, OX4 1RE, United Kingdom
Tel: (01865) 793806 Fax: (01865) 248780
email: info@howtobooks.co.uk
http://www.howtobooks.co.uk

First edition 2005

British Library Cataloguing in Publication Data
A catalogue record for this book is available from
the British Library.

Produced for How To Books by Deer Park Productions, Tavistock
Typeset by *specialist* publishing services ltd, Milton Keynes
Printed and bound by Cromwell Press, Trowbridge, Wiltshire

Note: The material contained in this book is set out in good
faith for general guidance and no liability can be accepted
for loss or expense incurred as a result of relying in particular
circumstances on statements made in the book. The laws and
regulations are complex and liable to change, and readers should
check the current position with the relevant authorities before
making personal arrangements.

Contents

Acknowledgements

Once again I would like to thank Joan Stock for her support and contribution, researching documents and checking the final manuscript for facts, omissions and errors.

The Story of Spain by Mark Williams and *The New Spaniards* by John Hooper provided an insight into recent social history. How the last 70 years has affected today's new foreigner and Spanish laws is solely my interpretation.

There were considerable resources available to assist in compiling this book. Most were outdated or inaccurate. However, requests were always answered promptly by the British Consulate in Spain and the Spanish Embassy in London.

Introduction

While most of Spain's visitors are transient, taking short-term holidays, some northern Europeans become temporary or permanent residents, settling mainly near the Mediterranean coast or on the Islands. An early trickle of migrants in the 1960s has now become a steady flow, making Spain one of the principal holiday homes and international retirement locations for people originating from northern Europe.

While climate is important, another reason for Spain's popularity is grounded in personal finances, as there are considerable house price differentials between northern and southern Europe. There are also lower living costs, cheaper food, reduced heating bills and lower taxes. A slower pace of life, feeling more relaxed and the opportunities for golf, sailing and active sports attract many. Some are influenced by the presence of a British community, a good social life and a friendly local population. All have a degree of antipathy to the UK and generally wish to live abroad for at least part of the year, or as long-term expatriates with no desire to return to the UK.

There are 250,000 ex-pats (a strange term suggesting that if they return home one day they will become pats again) along the 120km stretch of the Costa del Sol, with perhaps an even larger population along the Costa Blanca and as many as 100,000 who have made it to the Islands. With an additional 300,000 Spanish-home-owning, permanent holidaymakers you have a British ex-pat community rapidly approaching a million. These statistics are approximate, as a large percentage of people who own a property do not reside full-time in Spain and there are those who reside, but choose not to declare their presence in the country for tax purposes.

1

There is little information available to help newcomers deal with Spanish laws. Most rely on friends or books for information, but the real need is for detailed information in a country where contradictions are common. The law states that if you spend more than six months a year in Spain it is necessary to become a resident and pay taxes to Spain. But many do not! The law states that the market value of the house, or close to it, has to be declared in the deeds. But many do not! There are traffic laws, but these are ignored by tolerant police. Why? The answers to these conundrums are simple. There is the law and the application of a law, and the two can be different. A perplexed foreigner who erects a garden shed of three square meters in a garden of 640 square meters is told to remove it because it is against the law. But a local solicitor, who understands urban matters, obtains permission because they understand the law is one thing and its interpretation by an official at the town hall is a totally different matter.

Perplexity does not end there. A foreign property owner in Spain is confronted by the law from two countries upon considering inheritance – one country wants inheritance tax, yet accepts that another country's law will be followed for inheritance rules.

Spanish law is evolved by a history of codes, for it is not the common law of England and Wales based on precedent. It is strongly influenced by the last 70 years, where current law is set against the political and economic context of that period. The empty *fincas* of a rural housing market are a throwback to the 'years of hunger'. Religious influence binds together unusual inheritance laws and consequently strong family units. Tolerant policing is a function of delays in the legal system. Immigration regulations and laws about foreigners are a function of Spain's membership of the EU, where increased prosperity has also led to an influx of illegal immigrants from Morocco.

This is a book about the laws of Spain for readers who will probably buy a house and possibly a car. As a consequence they most certainty will deal with legal issues and definitely with some Spanish authorities. They will need to understand several forms of taxation and obey laws in a country with different customs and a different language. A tall order! To assist in this process this book does not deal with all Spanish law – that would be impossible. It describes procedures for essential tasks. It tells you when to go it alone, when to get advice and when it is necessary to stand back, allowing an expert to take over.

Harry King, Pedreguer, Spain

1
Historical Perspective

INTRODUCTION

First let's look at the impact of the last 70 years during which Spain changed from a war-torn economy to a modern democracy at the heart of Europe. Spain is a young country. It was 1976 when its constitutional structure was implemented and then only after years of hunger, poverty and deprivation.

This is not a historical account of Spain's many invaders, of faded monarchies, religious persecution, conquering warriors laden with tons of gold or shipwrecked armadas. To understand modern Spain there is a need only to have knowledge of its recent past, in particular the Civil War, the 40-year dictatorship of General Francisco Franco, a brief period before tourists arrived and its transition to a new democratic government.

Understanding this short history is one thing; appreciating its effect on modern Spain will become apparent in subsequent chapters of this book.

RECENT SOCIAL AND POLITICAL HISTORY

The civil war

Spain became a republic in 1931 when King Alfonso XIII suspended royal power and went into exile. Social and political tensions grew, along with economic problems. The accompanying confrontations between political factions finally erupted with a military uprising on 17 July 1936. Spain suddenly captured the world stage. It might have been just another of the many military uprisings characterising Spanish history, but this time the rebels received the immediate support of Hitler and Mussolini. The world took sides: Stalin lined up alongside the Popular Front government, which received only lukewarm support from France and Britain.

What could have been a failed coup thus led to a long war, in which an estimated one to two million Spaniards and thousands of foreign volunteers fought and died. The world interpreted the war as a struggle between fascism, communism and democracy, but it was first of all a civil war, in which the two faces of Spain confronted each other. Rural, nationalist, Catholic countrymen fought against urban Republicans. For three long years Spain's war foreshadowed the horrors of the Second World War.

In modern times no Western European country has known such a merciless, bloody purge as that of Franco in the aftermath of the war. A calculation of the number of death sentences carried out until the early 1940s varies from 28,000 to 150,000. This frightening number reflects a desire to annihilate an enemy rather than any eagerness for revenge; more a continuation of the war than the pursuance of any political peace. The dominance of a military element over a political civilian one corresponded to Franco's mentality. The regime was a carbon copy of Fascist regimes: finger printing people[1], the same ceremonies and the same institutional characteristics, a single party and a cooperative system.

Political feelings still run deep in Spain. Some Spaniards who fought in the civil war are still alive today. Many Spaniards lived out their lives in other countries rather than remain under Franco. Others stayed in Spain but suffered the brutal consequences of having been on the wrong side. As time passes, the combatants die off and a whole new generation exists who were was born after 1939. The Civil War

---

1. Applying for a *residencia* today still requires fingerprinting.

and the Franco era is the subject of many written memoirs but the entire episode sits uncomfortably in the minds of today's Spaniards, who rarely discuss it and who continue to be acutely aware that their democracy is still relatively young.

The years of hunger

During the Second World War Spain had remained neutral while actively favouring its old supporters, the Axis. At the end of the war Spain was in a strange position, not entitled to the rewards of victory nor at risk from the encroaching power of the Soviet Union. There was no incentive to give Spain aid and a very good reason for denying it. In fact the world powers punished Spain for supporting the Axis. In December 1946 the newly-created United Nations passed a resolution recommending a trade boycott. Coming on top of the deprivations brought about by the civil war, which had cut real income per capita to nineteenth-century levels, the boycott was a disaster for the country. While the rest of Europe benefited from the Marshall Plan, Spain did not. The Franco government was diplomatically isolated.

All of Europe suffered deprivation in the post-war era, but Spain[2], where the late 1940s are known as the years of hunger, suffered more than most. In the cities cats and dogs disappeared from the streets, having either starved to death or been eaten. In the countryside the poorer peasants lived off boiled grass and weeds. But for the loans granted by General Peron, the Argentine dictator, to purchase beef and cereals, it is possible there would have been a full-scale famine.

Spain was a dictatorship, but not a Communist one. Recognising the new enemy was Communism, Spain and the United States signed a mutual defence and aid treaty in 1953. Under this treaty four US bases were established in various parts of Spain, with about 12,000 military personnel. The issue was tied in with Spain's membership of NATO but, more importantly, it also legitimised Franco in the eyes of the world.

Although the UN blockade was lifted, inward looking policies continued to be pursued. In spite of promoting rural economy as the way forward, agricultural output fell to a level lower than at the end of the civil war. Industry, insulated from the outside world by tariffs and quotas, was unable to buy the foreign technology it needed to modernise and could only grow at a painfully slow pace. National income

---

2. Today sons and daughters are often taller and thinner than their parents or grandparents whose stunted growth occurred in the years of hunger.

did not regain its pre-civil war level until 1951 and it was not until 1954 that the average income returned to the point it had reached in 1936.

To the villagers in Andalusia, which had been the scene of desperate poverty even before the civil war, the deprivations of the post-war era were the final straw. Individuals, families and in some cases entire villages packed up their belongings and headed for the industrial centres of the north. Once they reached the cities, migrants settled on the outskirts. With nowhere else to live, they built shacks out of whatever they could scavenge. The shacks were suffocating in summer and bitterly cold in the winter. None had running water.

Franco's regime was bankrupt in thought and deed. The foreign exchange account was in the red, inflation was heading into double figures and there were serious signs of unrest for the first time since the war. It took a long time to persuade Franco that a radical change was required. Enter a new breed in Spanish politics – the technocrat, who came from a well-to-do background, had had a distinguished career in academic or professional life and belonged to, or sympathised with, the secretive Catholic fellowship, Opus Dei.

Economic revival

It was not until two years after their appointment that the new team of technocrats began their assault on the economy. Their short-term aim was to tackle inflation and redress the balance of payments. Public spending was cut, credit was curbed, wages were frozen, overtime was restricted and the *peseta* devalued. The economic revival was underway. Prices levelled out and the deficit in the balance of payments was transformed into a surplus by the end of the following year.

However the cost in human misery was considerable as real earnings were again slashed. As a result, many Spaniards set off to find work abroad. During the late 1950s and into the 1960s well over a million Spaniards emigrated to Germany, France, Britain and other European countries. A rising standard of living in those countries created jobs which their own nationals were unwilling to fill, but were attractive to people from the poor farming and fishing villages of Spain.

Spain was opened up to foreign investment, much of the red tape binding industry was cut, restrictions were lifted on imports and incentives were offered for exports. Years of development followed. Economic performance improved dramatically. Between 1961 and 1973 the economy grew at seven per cent a year. Income per head quadrupled, removing Spain from the ranks of the developing nations. By the time Spain's economic miracle had ended, she was the world's ninth industrial power. The wealth generated by her progress led to a substantial improvement in standards of living. Spaniards had a better diet, their physical growth no longer stunted. The number of homes with a washing-machine and a refrigerator leapt. Car ownership increased. Telephones ceased to be the prerogative of offices. The number of university students tripled.

The 1960s

Tourism had been growing steadily throughout the 1950s but it was not until 1959, when the government abolished visas for holidaymakers from Western Europe, that tourism really took off. In the 1960s sunny Spain, where the weather was good and prices were low, became a prime vacation spot for Northern Europeans. The £20 long holiday weekend was born. The material benefits of the tourist boom were considerable – not only for property developers, but also for shopkeepers and the ordinary people of the villages near the coast who became waiters and chambermaids in tourist hotels. This development took place in an environment which had not changed very much since the eighteenth century – a world of thrift and deprivation which had its own strict moral code. Overnight Spaniards, accustomed to watching almonds grow, were confronted with a new way of life in which it seemed visiting men had more money than they could spend and women walked around virtually naked. A new way of life was born.

The economic miracle changed but did not stop internal migration. Poverty stricken villagers from Andalusia continued to move into the cities. They were joined by increasing numbers from Galicia and the interior regions. The typical migrant of the 1950s – a labourer forced to move by hunger – was joined by a farmer who was unable to make a living from the soil, a craftsman and a shopkeeper whose standards of living had dropped because of the falling population in the countryside.

Come the 1960s, the original migrants were beginning to move out of their shanty towns and into cheap high-rise accommodation. Since shack-building was by then practically impossible, the new arrivals either had to buy a shack from a family which was moving on to better things or pay for accommodation in the apartment of a family which had already done so. From the point of view of the first wave of migrants, selling a shack became a way of getting the down payment on a flat.

While cities were rapidly becoming overcrowded, the countryside was becoming depopulated. Today it is possible to come upon evidence of deserted hamlets or abandoned towns which harkens back to another age like nowhere else in Europe. Perhaps the most forlorn are those that are almost, but not quite, abandoned – where the inhabitants are too old to leave[3]. The population was polarised. At one end there was Barcelona, as crowded as any industrial centre of North Western Europe, and at the other there were provinces with fewer inhabitants per square kilometer than an African country.

The 1970s

The miracle ended with the same dramatic suddenness with which it had begun. The European boom had started to run out of steam towards the end of the 1960s and the first people to feel the effects were the emigrants. As the expansion of other Western European economies began to slow down, the number of jobs available declined and the need for foreign labour diminished. After 1970 the number of Spaniards leaving the country to work abroad dropped off. Those who were already working abroad began to find that they were no longer required. Even so, Spain's invisible earnings would have been enough to cover her trade deficit had it not been for the increase in oil prices following the war in the Middle East. The OPEC price rises doubled the size of Spain's trade gap and unleashed the inflationary pressures that had been simmering away below the surface of the economy throughout the boom years.

Then, on 20 November 1975, General Franco died and the Spanish nation was left with the task of restoring democracy in the depths of a worldwide recession. For 38 years all the important decisions had been taken by one man. Until his dying day, Franco had restricted power to those who had refused to countenance change, or accepted the need for change but were only prepared to introduce it slowly and conditionally. If Spain were to change it was clear that much would depend on the role played by the young man who had succeeded Franco.

---

3. Houses abandoned in the 1960s are now the eagerly sought *fincas* of today's foreign invaders.

The return of the King

Two days after Franco's death in 1975, his heir and protégé was crowned – Juan Carlos I, El Rey de España. His first duty was to attend Franco's state funeral at the Valley of the Fallen, the vast mausoleum hacked from rock which commemorates the dead of the Spanish Civil War, and where many are interred. Juan Carlos was not someone in whom Spaniards had much faith. Ever since the age of ten the young Prince had been projected by the media as a loyal son of the regime, completing his education with distinction and going on to attend all three military academies. He had rarely been seen except in Franco's shadow, standing behind the old dictator on platforms and podiums at official ceremonies. The overall impression was of a nice enough chap but with not enough intelligence or imagination to question the conventions of his background. Few people can have been as misjudged as Juan Carlos, for his rather gauche manner belied a penetrating and receptive mind.

Under the constitutional system devised by Franco, the monarch could only choose his Prime Minister from a list of three names drawn up by the Council of the Realm, a 17-man advisory body consisting almost entirely of Franco diehards. Knowing that he stood no chance of getting a suitable candidate from the Council, the King reluctantly reconfirmed Carlos Arias Navarro as Prime Minister. An uncharismatic lawyer, Arias was aware that the nation was clamouring for democracy but he was temperamentally and ideologically committed to a dictatorship. Arias was incapable of moving either forwards or backwards. He outlined a programme of limited reforms but made things worse with a broadcast to the nation in which he seemed to be living in the past. A bill for the legalisation of political parties was passed by parliament but hours later the same assembly threw out the legislation needed to put it into effect. The incident showed that Arias could not even carry with him his old friends and colleagues from the Franco establishment. The King called him to the palace and told him the situation was unacceptable. Arias had never really enjoyed being Prime Minister and seized the opportunity to tender his resignation which the King accepted at once.

The birth of a nation

When the King's new choice eventually became known, the reaction was stunned disbelief. The man he had chosen to succeed Arias was Adolfo Suarez, who at 43 was the youngest member of the outgoing government. Everything about Suarez except his youth seemed to be at variance with the spirit of the times. He had spent his entire working life serving the dictator in a variety of posts. Not surprisingly, he filled his first government with men of his own age whom he had met on his way up through the state system. 'What a mistake! What an immense mistake!' declared one of Spain's leading newspapers of the day.

The King's choice of Suarez was the culmination of months of conspiracy. During the last months of Franco's life, Juan Carlos had asked a number of politicians and officials for their opinions on how the country could best be transformed. One of the most detailed and realistic appraisals came from Suarez who seemed to fulfil the requirements of a Prime Minister whose job it would be to change Spain from a dictatorship into a democracy. He had an intimate knowledge of the workings of the administration, accepted that reform could not be partial or gradual and had enough charisma to survive once democracy had been restored. From a middle class background he was affable and thoroughly versed in the use of the media.

Suarez moved fast. Three months after the swearing-in of his government, he had laid before the Cortes (Spanish parliament) a political reform bill which introduced universal suffrage and a two-chamber parliament, consisting of a lower house, or Congress, and an upper house to be called the Senate. To ease its passage it was made clear to members of the Cortes that the way they voted would affect such matters as who would sit on which committee and whether a blind eye would be turned to certain untaxed accounts. The entire proceedings were broadcast on radio and television and all the deputies were called upon by name to stand up and say either yes or no to reform. One by one the members of the Cortes, generals and admirals, ex-ministers, bankers and local bigwigs stood up and endorsed a measure that would put an end to everything they had spent their lives supporting. Spaniards realised that the long nightmare of Franco had really come to an end.

Reform and revolt

Further reform measures came thick and fast. The cabinet endorsed a procedure for the legalisation of political parties. The Socialists were legalised first, and then the Communists, the right to strike was recognised and trade unions were legalised. Then the government and opposition parties agreed on how the elections should be conducted and votes counted. A new constitution was agreed[4]. A new, democratic country was born.

A few years later, after a distinguished term in office, Adolfo Suarez resigned. Only days later Spain faced its greatest challenge, and Juan Carlos his finest hour. In the late afternoon of 23 February 1981, Leopoldo Calvo Sotelo was about to be installed as Spain's new Prime Minister when suddenly the doors to the Cortes were flung open to admit Lieutenant Colonel Antonio Tejero and a large force of armed Guardia Civil. The entire Cortes was placed in custody. In Valencia, General Milans de Bosch declared a state of emergency and ordered tanks onto the streets. Spain was again within a hair's breadth of a military *coup d'état*.

With all the elected members of Parliament held in the Cortes, only one man stood between Spain and a return to military rule. Had Juan Carlos panicked and fled the capital, it would have been all over for Spain's democracy. But El Rey was made of sterner stuff. Summoning a television crew to La Zarzuela, his private home, Juan Carlos donned full uniform as Commander-in-Chief of the Spanish forces, and broadcast direct to the nation, ordering all units of the armed forces to take whatever steps were necessary to restore democracy. Spain breathed a great sigh of relief, and within hours the attempted coup was over. This, to some an embarrassingly comic interlude, consigned the generals to oblivion.

The 1980s

One of the first acts the new Gonzales government was the ill-advised Worker's Statute in 1984 which laid down long holidays and highly restrictive labour policies that virtually guaranteed lifetime job security to employees[5]. This acted as a disincentive to employers who feared rocketing labour costs. As a result, many companies stopped hiring and unemployment climbed to 20 per cent, far and away Europe's highest. Twenty-five per cent were officially working in the black economy while collecting government benefits.

Yet by 1986 it was clear that things were generally working. The economy was showing good signs as inflation fell, productivity rose and the huge budget deficit became a surplus. Under the Socialists democracy was firmly consolidated, the

---

4. A brief outline of the new constitution is contained in Chapter 2.
5. See Chapter 13 – Working in Spain.

military modernised and partly removed from the shadows. The Socialist government launched major development programmes in agriculture and tourism and rebuilt the infrastructure, especially the nation's crumbling road system. With the economy improving steadily, money began pouring into government coffers. It seemed a new golden age had arrived.

Yet the movement from countryside to cities continued to give Spain the highest percentage of apartment dwellers in Europe. Conversely, rural areas became markedly underpopulated. The numbers employed in agriculture fell dramatically. Those who lived in rural areas were still poor and illiterate.

However the new urbanised Spaniard was delighted by the temptations of modern consumer society, from cell phones to Seat cars, as if trying to quickly acquire those things denied them under the old regime. By the late 1980s Spaniards had some of the world's highest disposable incomes and enjoyed longer life expectancies than Americans and Britons. Times had changed.

Socially the sexual revolution of the 1980s was described by Spaniards themselves as 'a binge'. Kerb side vending machines sold condoms, and prostitutes named their offering and price in the classified ad sections of the press. Gays and lesbians surfaced openly for the first time. Abortion rates rocketed – one for every two live births, the highest in the western world. The Catholic nation that once led Europe in high birthrates now had just 1.5 children per family. London of the swinging 60s happened in Madrid around 1985[6].

Scandal

The first civilian head of the Guardia Civil was caught stealing from secret funds used to pay informants and the widows of slain policemen. The director of the Bank of Spain was locked up for financial irregularities. Suspicious links were shown between the interior ministry and a group of off-duty policemen thought responsible for numerous deaths of suspected ETA (*Euzkadi Ta Azkatasuna*) terrorists resulting in the interior minister going to jail. Yet few offenders from the power elite were ever punished for corruption. Spaniards became increasingly cynical. Respect for the law was at an all time low[7]. Delay in law seemed normal but it was now avoidance that

---

6. Twenty years on, the mainstream press carries adverts for sexual services. The birth rate is low and Spain's abortion laws are still the most restrictive in Europe.
7. Chapter 2 expands further on Spaniards' disrespect for the law.

hit a new standard. In a nation with such a large underground economy, tax evasion and fraud became a national sport.

Entry into the EU

Approval was gained for a phased entry to the EU in 1986 with full membership by 1992. No other nation seemed so enthusiastic over the idea of a united Europe as Spain. The nation's acceptance of foreign leadership reflected a mistrust of Madrid and Spanish politicians. This romance with Europeanism was a complex affair revealing deeply ingrained national traits – a desire to belong to something other than traditional Spain.

Entry into the EU helped create boom days as foreign money poured into the Spanish economy which again enjoyed the fastest growth rate in Europe. The end of trade barriers and government control was like a breath of fresh air, and for several years Madrid's stock market was the most active and profitable in the world.

There was a down side. Imports flooded into the country and exports dropped, a textbook example of what happens to a protected economy when it enters a free market. By the end of the decade, international interests owned all six of Spain's car manufacturers; foreigners soon controlled eight of the top ten chemical companies; and multinationals moved in on a grand scale.

Spain's producers, faced with foreign competition for the first time, suffered. In particular the Basque region was burdened with outdated traditional industry – coal, steel, shipbuilding – that had fallen on hard times. Factories were in dire need of modernisation if they hoped to remain competitive, yet foreign investors were wary of the Basque region and its political problems.

Conversely Barcelona, well placed to serve the huge European market, was reaping great benefits from EU membership. Some Catalans began speaking of a Europe of regions rather than nations and had their own lobby in Brussels. Indeed, all Spain was delighted with the huge amounts of cash available for roads, airports and other public projects.

Internationally Spain's role in world affairs continued to change. No longer would it sit on its hands and watch. The government allowed former US bases to be used as critical staging areas for the Gulf War of 1990. Spain re-emerged as an important diplomatic force in the Americas through its peacekeeping efforts in Nicaragua, El Salvador and Guatemala. It also played a role in the Balkan conflict. Now a stable Spain could lend a hand as Yugoslavia disintegrated into civil war not unlike its own nightmare decades earlier.

1992

Spain's prestige abroad was at its highest as 1992 began. The nation was obsessed with showing its best face. Large-scale public works transformed highways and airports, and a new bullet-train between Seville and Madrid was launched. To commemorate the discovery of America five centuries previously, the city of Seville played host to a colossal international exposition called Expo-92. In the same year Barcelona was home to a highly successful Olympic Games and used the occasion for extensive urban renewal. Not to be outdone, Madrid presented a non-stop series of events as Cultural Capital of Europe.

1992 also marked a decade in power for Gonzalez and the Socialists, far longer than any previous elected government in Spain. There was good reason to celebrate. During the Socialists' tenure Spain shook off decades of isolation from the rest of Europe. The bloody past of Spanish history had been laid to rest. Clerics and generals were gone from the stage. Regionalism gave way to rational autonomy. ETA was on the wane.

However at the end of 1992 the world economic crisis was having serious effects on the Spanish economy. There were signs that the long national fiesta was over. The Madrid stock market declined 30 per cent in a year. Economists warned that the nation was living beyond its means and could no longer consume far more than it produced.

1992 and on

Regional autonomy had greatly swollen the ranks of Spanish bureaucracy. In the ten years to 1992, the number of civil servants working in the 17 regional governments increased dramatically. Catalonia was a virtual state within a state with tens of thousands of public employees. Part of the endemic labour problem stemmed from society's attitudes to work itself. It seemed too many Spaniards dreamed of having a safe, paper-shuffling job in a government office. This affinity for secure, cushy office jobs reflected the deep-seated attitudes of Spaniards[8].

Spain needed desperately to create wealth, yet unemployment remained high with huge segments of the population standing idle. Instead of the free soup of 40 years ago, many were now receiving regular welfare cheques. The government itself was going broke with a vast cradle-to-grave social system modelled on its wealthier neighbours. In 1994, when public spending peaked at close to 50 per cent of the GDP, about 12 million persons were employed and 9.3 million received social benefits.

Facing the problem head on, the government focused on a key competitive weakness: the high cost of labour. Over the years Franco, Socialist governments and the unions had priced Spain out of the labour market. The Socialists decided to dismantle their own creation (the Workers Statute of 1984) before it was too late[9].

Yet Spain needed a more fundamental change. Tinkering at the edges was playing with the problem. The leader of the opposition party was José Maria Aznar. Small of stature and mild mannered, he had played no role in the post-Franco transition. He was the first national figure to come of age in the new Spain. Slowly gaining supporters, his popularity soared after he survived an ETA car bomb attack. Aznar was sworn in as the fourth premier of Spain. Twenty years after Franco's death, conservatives and not Socialists were finally accepted as a legitimate political force.

The new Prime Minister promised an austere programme of spending cuts and financial reforms, two years of sacrifice to meet strict EC guidelines for joining the monetary union. Aznar's agenda included major reductions in the civil service and mass privatisation of state-run companies. The nation was ready for Aznar's honest, business-like style. It was time for a pause and fortunately Spain's economy bounced back and remained vibrant throughout the decade. With these strides Spain formed part of the core group to launch the Euro in 1999.

---

8. Bureaucracy is still a problem in everyday life. It is getting better. Readers of this book will still be surprised at some of its procedures.
9. See Chapter 13 – Working in Spain.

MODERN SPAIN

We move into the new millennium. Up to 2004 three Prime Ministers held power since the restoration of democracy – Suarez, Gonzalez and Aznar. Looking back we can see that Suarez managed the transition of the country during the formative years of democracy. Gonzalez steered the country to obtain membership of the EU in 1986, thus ensuring Spain's economic growth which has benefitted greatly from the EU programme of special economic aid to poorer countries. Aznar tackled the budget deficit, provoking some discontent with resultant strikes but maintaining the country's strong economic ties with Europe.

Then the Madrid train bombings occurred in 2004, rocking the country. Eleven bombs wrecked four trains, killing 191 people and injuring hundreds. Spain was back to centre stage in Europe yet again. Grief and shock returned a Socialist government ill prepared for office. Terrorism suddenly hit Spain as its European neighbours looked on. Zapatero, the newly elected Prime Minister, dealt with the aftermath of the train bombings – coming to terms with the pacifist, no-war culture of Spain's people, created by their lingering memories of Franco.

Although the Madrid attacks were identified beyond all doubt as the work of fundamentalist terrorists, it spurred on the authorities to deal with ETA. 'ETA – how much longer?' was the cry. In late 2004 senior members of ETA were arrested in the Basque region of France, their hiding ground since 1975. Have the problems of ETA been put to rest?

Spain today

In 30 years Spain has achieved what has taken some countries centuries, transforming her political and social structure into that of a conventional Western democracy. A plethora of elections – general, regional, municipal as well as regional referenda – has gone some way to placating the aspirations of the Catalans, if not so much those of the Basques. Her democracy is established and although there may be some rough edges, her economy is at least no worse than many other western nations, and better than some. Prominent Spaniards have made the step into EU politics, and Spaniards are active at all levels of the EU administration. Greater visibility and prestige have also accrued from Spain's presidency of the EU and from international peace conferences held in Madrid. These developments, particularly on the political and economic front, are a source of pride for Spaniards. Spain is now a developed European country rather than just a backward 'sun and cheap wine' vacation spot.

Spain's relations with other countries are friendly, with no outstanding bones of contention, except perhaps Gibraltar. Spain may have her differences with her old adversary over The Rock, but they are polite, diplomatic differences. Spain's economy is sound, her society stable. She has, for the first time in her turbulent history, many friends amongst the international community. Her people remain as vibrant, as loyal and as individual as they ever were. Her national character remains unchanged, moulded by her turbulent history. Spain's democracy is still young, but it is strong, fixed and under good leadership.

FURTHER READING

Jimmy Burns, *When Beckham Went to Spain*. London: Penguin. Cleverly, through the story of *Real Madrid* and David Beckham, the reader learns about changes in Spain.

Justin Wintle, *The Rough Guide History of Spain*. London: Rough Guides, 2003.

2
Law and Order

INTRODUCTION

Spain follows a system of legal codes different from English common law. One is a written set of rules and the other is based on precedent. In 1978 a new Spanish Constitution came into being and included a set of values unheard of in the Franco era: a new structure to govern the country, a new judicial system and new liberal laws bringing with it tolerant policing. Over the subsequent years additional legalisation has been enacted including entry into the EU and a need to deal with the problems of illegal Moroccan immigrants.

No system is perfect. Are Spain's laws applied with alacrity or do abnormal delays lead to disrespect for the law itself? Does excessive officialdom breed avoidance of the law and does avoidance, tolerated to a degree, create an indifferent attitude to authority? In a decentralised structure of government do local councils ignore regional or national laws and furthermore does the government ignore EU rulings?

SPANISH CIVIL CODE

A code in jurisprudence is a systematic compilation of law in written form, issued by rulers in former times, and promulgated by legislative authorities after a rise of

18

representative governments. Early legal codes were little more than statements which had obtained the force of law in civilised communities. Of all the old codes, that of the Roman emperor Justinian I and known as the Justinian Code most closely resembles the codes of later times. The influence of the Justinian Code was great. Long after Rome fell, Roman law continued to serve as a source of law in Europe in the form of civil law. The Code Napoleon followed, being a balance between German, French and Roman law of Justinian I. Among the merits of the French code are its simplicity and clarity. As a result of the Napoleonic conquests, the code was introduced into a number of European countries and it became the model for the civil codes of today's Spain.

A modern code is designed to provide a comprehensive statement of the laws in force in a single branch of law, in a logical and convenient arrangement and in a precise, unambiguous phraseology. Modern codes include codes of civil, criminal, and public law, and codes of civil and criminal procedures. Statesmen of modern times have regarded legal codes as necessary instruments of national unity and central authority.

Attempts at defining a code of international public and private law have been unsuccessful. The League of Nations failed in its attempt to do so. The United Nations has established a commission to study the possible codification of various aspects of international law.

Civil law is a term applied to the body of private law used in countries in which the legal system is based on Roman law as modified by modern influences. Civil law is used in most nations in Europe, including Spain and partly Scotland but excluding England and Wales. The term 'civil law' is also employed to distinguish those legal codes that deal with civil relationships (such as citizenship, marriage, divorce, and certain contractual arrangements) from other codes such as those dealing with criminal law and maritime law.

English common law differs from civil law in origin and other important respects. In civil law, judicial interpretations are based primarily on a system of codified written law, rather than on the rule of precedent which is emphasised in the common law. The law of evidence, so important in common-law countries, has no counterpart in the civil law. The differences between civil law and common law, however, should not be overstated. Despite divergences in methods and terminology, a basic similarity is found in the ultimate results reached by both systems.

It is obvious that the legal system of Spain differs from that of the constituent countries of the UK. All Spanish law must now be formulated in accordance with the Spanish constitution of 1978. A constitutional court can strike out or amend an old law or code which it finds unconstitutional and will frequently do so.

SPANISH CONSTITUTION

Following the death of Franco and the re-emergence of democracy on 31 October 1978 the Spanish Parliament adopted a new written Constitution. It received the approval of the Spanish people in a referendum held on 6 December 1978 and became law when signed by King Juan Carlos on 27 December 1978.

The rights and obligations of all citizens of Spain are set out in considerable detail in 46 articles and can be viewed in full on www.igsap.map.es/cia/dispo/ce_ingles_index.htm. Thirty years later the contents look very basic for a modern European country, but in the aftermath of Franco's reign they were the words of democracy. In addition to the fundamental rights of equality before law – free speech, religious, ideological and cultural freedom – there are five Articles of particular interest, which are summarised below.

- **Article 10**. The dignity of the individual, free development of personality, respect for the law and for the rights of others is declared to be fundamental. The law is in conformity with the Universal Declaration of Human Rights and such other treaties which will protect these rights and freedoms and international agreements as may be ratified by Spain.

- **Article 15**. No one shall be tortured, chastised or submitted to inhuman or degrading treatment. The death penalty will be abolished, except under military law in time of war.

- **Article 17**. No one can be deprived of liberty except in the circumstances and in the manner laid down by law. Preventative detention shall last only for so long as may be strictly necessary to elucidate the facts of a case, and in all cases a person must be released or brought before a court within 72 hours. Anyone kept in custody must be informed immediately and in a manner they can understand their rights and the reason for their detention. They are not obliged to make any statement and are entitled to the assistance of a lawyer in all judicial and police enquiries. The law accepts the principle of *Habeas Corpus*.

- **Article 18**. A person and family is entitled to the right to privacy. Without consent a home cannot be entered or searched, except under a judicial warrant or when a serious crime has been committed.

- **Article 24**. Everyone has the right of access to the courts, to be defended by a lawyer, to be informed of any charges made against them and to have the protection of a public hearing without undue delay. They can bring evidence in their defence, refuse to make any statement which might incriminate them, and are presumed innocent until proved guilty.

GOVERNING SPAIN

The 1978 constitution restored some identity to the ancient kingdoms and regions which originally made up the nation in 1492. The result was a kind of United States of Spain. It is a tightly regulated country having five levels of government. The top two levels comprise a Congress and Senate of elected representatives from the provinces, the Islands and the regions. The main focus of government lies with 17 autonomous regions, called *Comunidades*, each with their own parliament. The autonomous regions are further divided into *Provinces* and then into the smaller *Municipio*.

It is a unique system – a variable degree of decentralisation giving autonomy to the *Comunidades* an acknowledgement of Spain's troubled past, yet centralised in order to control common interests such as defence and its relationship with the EU.

ATTITUDES TO TAX, DELAY, OFFICIALDOM AND LAW

While history, government and Spain's institutions set a framework, some tolerance has to be made for flaws in any system. Having seen their homeland change rapidly from a war torn dictatorship to a thriving, democratic and successful part of the EU in a period of 70 years, how has this left Spain's citizens? Pacifist and abhorrent of war! Tolerant of most things! Proud and hard working! And their attitude to authority? To be dealt with patiently, respectfully and anticipating delay. In many ways the Spanish character is at ease with defects found in their legal system. All these facets affect a Spaniard's way of behaving for they will interpret the law according to their own perception. If their perception is of delay, bureaucracy and avoidance then that is precisely how they will respond.

Tax – to pay or not to pay

The first step towards a unified tax system was taken in 1977. A few months after the first general election the Finance Minister steered through the *Cortes* an elementary tax reform law. It unified a system of income tax so that wage earners and non-wage earners were assessed according to the same rules. For the first time tax evasion was made an offence.

The next step was to increase the number of people who had to fill in tax returns. In 1980, for the first time, anyone who earned more than a certain amount, or who owned a house worth more than a certain amount, or a car of less than a certain age, or who employed more than one servant, or had a seat on a board of directors, had to fill in a tax return.

In 1990 the government appeared to recognise the limits of its ability to clamp down on evasion when it offered an amnesty. Tax-dodgers were given a choice between declaring their black money free of the threat of a penalty, or investing it in a new series of special, low-interest government securities. The move brought to light 1,700 billion *pesetas*. The share of fiscal revenue in gross domestic product reached 34 per cent, a 13 per cent improvement on 1977 but still below a European average of 39 per cent.

Tax evasion however, by those who have the opportunity to practise it, is still rife today. According to a study a third of the income earned in Spain is undeclared. It is still common for companies to keep two sets of accounts. The President of the Spanish employers' federation described evasion as an 'entrepreneurial necessity'. As for taxes on the buying and selling of property, it is thought that on average parties to a transaction declare about two-thirds of the real price when a house is new, and only a half if it is not.

The government's failure to curb these abuses, and the *Haciendia* (income tax office) turning a blind eye to 'black money', explains why the poorest contribute a disproportionate amount of tax as it comes from those who do not have the opportunity to fiddle: the country's wage and salary earners who have tax deducted at source. More importantly it makes a statement that, within reason, income tax avoidance is accepted and tolerated.

Disrespect through delay and cost

While no one disputes the validity of Spanish law and fairness of its judicial system, many question the innumerable delays which inevitably cause social issues far beyond mere frustration. In 1983 more than 80 people died in a fire at a Madrid disco but it took ten years for the case to reach trial. In 1982 a dam burst in the east of Spain, damaging or destroying the property of almost 25,000 people, but it was not until 1993 that any of the victims received compensation. In 1981 adulterated cooking oil killed more than 600 people and afflicted another 25,000. The main hearing was held in 1989, but the cases against senior government officials accused of negligence took many more years to resolve.

The most unacceptable result of delay in a legal system is the disrespect it breeds for the law itself. Ignore planning regulations, fail to pay a fine, debt or rent and there is a very good chance of getting away with it, because the other party will find it is not worth the time or effort of pursuing the issue. Better to settle out of court, or drop the case because it will take so long.

And there is the cost! Nobody pays a parking fine. The chances of a council pursuing the issue through the courts to the point where the individual will pay are slight. It is far more sensible to throw the ticket in the nearest bin and forget about it. Hence the double and triple parked cars which line busy streets, cars parked on pavements, cars parked everywhere. This ultimately leads to tolerant policing.

Look at beautiful stretches of the Spanish coastline or rolling hillsides and you will find dozens of properties that no planning officer has approved. By the time the council had obtained an injunction, the work was done. And since no one has the heart to order a demolition, especially if the owner wields some influence in the area, the most that is likely to happen is that he or she will have to pay a fine. The length and breadth of Spain there are hundreds of homes, blocks of flats or even urbanisations which nobody has ever agreed should be there.

The bottle neck in judicial machinery has given birth to a Spaniard who is an opportunist, living off their wits, one step ahead of their creditors. It is easily done. Sign a contract for a one-year rental for an apartment and then don't pay the rent. Let the owners go to court to regain their property and get their lost rent. When the going gets hot, move on and do it all over again. Knowledgeable perpetrators of fraud ask the question 'So what are you going to do then, sue me?' Sometimes it may be better to deal with the matter personally, such as changing locks on an apartment door and depositing personal possessions on the pavement. No one wishes to disobey the law but sometimes it is expedient to deal with justice personally, which is exactly what a judicial system is designed to avoid.

Breeding avoidance

While it is not necessary to obtain permission to wallpaper a room, Spanish officialdom can be all pervasive. When something has to be done, approved or achieved it usually follows a standard pattern – fill in a form and get it approved. It all takes time.

First, there is a queue for the application form. Then a queue to hand it in, only to find the application is not valid unless accompanied by two other documents which can only be obtained from other departments in different parts of town. Once obtained queue again only to discover that the application will not take effect until stamped by the head of department and he has gone home for the day.

The whole process is made more difficult by the opening hours of the little grilles behind which Spanish bureaucrats confront their public. Not only can the opening hours vary from department to department, but they are always as short as possible. Then there are the fiestas, local and national holidays! Anything of importance could take weeks or months.

What does this achieve? It breeds avoidance. Rather than stand in a long queue – let's not bother. Rather than go through a long planning application – let's just get on with the job. Hopefully the reputation of Spanish officialdom may be historic as things are now changing fast, with many services highly computerised. Consequently it soon may not be possible for Spain's citizens to hide behind the suffocating blanket of bureaucracy.

A blind eye from Councils and *Comunidades*

Let's move forward to 2005. Spain's new Socialist government has vowed to demolish illegally built houses and hotels in an attempt to preserve the parts of its coastline that remain unspoilt. Determined to prevent the Costas from disappearing entirely beneath concrete, a raft of measures was announced to protect the country's 8,000-mile coastline. Chief among them is a commitment to enforce a 1988 law that banned the construction of any building within 100 metres of the shore and which is conveniently ignored by local planning authorities. This initiative would guarantee public access to the entire coast, its recovery and transformation in spoilt and built-up areas. The government appears to have been spurred into action by a series of reports decrying the toll taken by excessive development. One study claimed that unchecked construction of hotels, houses and marinas, but approved by local authorities, had helped to blight 90 per cent of the coast.

Land law

Concern has also been growing over the effects of a controversial land law in the Valencia region, which has not only fuelled overdevelopment but has financially crippled thousands of homeowners, including many Britons. The law, known as *La Ley Reguladora de la Actividad Urbanistica*, was introduced in 1994, ostensibly to regulate the acquisition and development of land and prevent excessive speculation.

However, a report by the European Parliament stated it had been misused by unscrupulous developers to force homeowners to sell their homes at well below market prices, or to make them pay excessive sums towards the cost of local infrastructure. 'There is no doubt that the application of the land law has led to a serious abuse of the most elementary rights of many thousands of European citizens, either by design or by deceit,' the report concluded. 'They have had their land and their homes expropriated, and had to pay for the experience, finding themselves in a surreal legal environment without any proper recourse to legal justice.'

Bewilderment

A citizen of Spain is subject to laws set at European, national and regional level. So too are many countries but in decentralised Spain they may be applied, interpreted, or ignored at all these levels. They may be applied to the letter or with latitude, depending who is involved. All this creates law and an application of law as two different things.

Bewilderment is created for a new foreigner who has to tread carefully in a country where he or she does not understand its attitudes. Accustomed to a more formal and stricter application of regulations in northern Europe they are lost in the informal 'ducking and diving' that takes place in Spain.

Spaniards themselves take to this fluidity like ducks to water, knowing all the ins and outs, not hesitating to take full advantage of any loophole offered. It is their way of life, quite a natural thing to do, a lifestyle characteristic.

The two cultures often meet when completing a commercial transaction such as building a house. One side is accustomed to formality, order and trust, the other is bred on informality, latitude and taking a degree of advantage. In order to bring the two cultures together books like this are written, always advising foreigners to check, tie things down in writing and if in doubt check again, not with friends who may be unintentionally wrong, but with an unbiased *abogado* (lawyer).

RECENT LAW

It is not necessary to understand the Spanish Civil Code or for that matter the Constitution – that is now the role of the judiciary – but on the other hand there is one recent law of interest, the *Ley de Derechos y Libertades de los Extranjeros en Espana* (Law for the Rights and Freedoms of Foreigners in Spain). This law first appeared in 1985, was changed in 2000 and modified one year later. It is of particular interest to a foreigner living in Spain, many clauses influencing the contents of this book.

Two factors impinge on Spain's treatment of foreigners. The first is the requirement of free movement of citizens within the EU and the second is a contrary pressure on how to deal with the massive influx of illegal immigrants from North Africa. How is this done? The law has now greatly simplified procedures for allowing EU citizens to settle and work in Spain, so much so that new residents enjoy equal rights to Spaniards. And the Moroccans? Periodic amnesties have been granted to legalise their situation, enabling them to obtain work permits together with access to health care services.

POLICE

Spain has three main police forces, often with overlapping roles: local municipal police, the national police and the civil guard. They are all armed and should be treated with appropriate respect. Some regions, including the Basque area and Catalonia, have their own police forces. An elite special operations group is responsible for combating terrorism and guarding Spanish ambassadors and embassies abroad. Other forces include port police and armed guards employed by banks and security companies.

Municipal Police

Municipal police, referred to as *Policia Local,* are attached to the local town hall. They wear blue uniforms with white checked bands on their hats and sleeves, and patrol in white or blue cars or even on motor scooters. Municipal police deal with minor crime such as parking offences, civil disturbances and the enforcement of local laws. They control traffic and protect property.

National Police

Stationed in large towns the *Policia Nacional* deal with serious crime such as robbery, murder and muggings. Other duties include guarding embassies, railway stations, post offices, army barracks and controlling demonstrations. They are housed in a conventional police station, some of which have an *extranjeros* (foreigners) department which deals with *residencia* cards and other matters relating to foreigners such as controlling illegal immigrants.

Civil Guard

The *Guardia Civil* patrol Spain's highways in pairs, on motorcycles or in cars. They mainly deal with traffic offences and road accidents, but also act as immigration officers and frontier guards. In villages too small for a national police station, the *Guardia Civil* stand in for all duties. These motorcycle policemen wear a green uniform assisting motorists in difficulty, but more likely stopping vehicles to check papers or to inform a motorist of an impending speeding fine.

Spanish police are generally tolerant and extremely helpful. Of course it is to be hoped that no major problems will arise and the worst encounter might be a fine for a traffic offence. If this happens the police will fill in a short report and can fine a non-resident on the spot. Drivers must have personal identification, driving licence and all car documents to hand. Some people resent carrying such valuable documents in a car and may well be excused for not carrying them. But it is illegal to be without at least a copy and it can be a real nuisance if the police insist on seeing them.

Basque Country and Catalonia

The two regions with the greatest autonomy have their own autonomous police forces, called the *Ertxaintxa* and the *Mossos d'Escuadra*. Eventually they may assume the functions of the *Policia Nacional* and *Guardia Civil* in their respective communities but, for the time being, they co-exist with national forces. The *Mossos* have taken over rural and highway policing from the Guardia Civil in many parts of Catalonia.

Denuncia

If you have a complaint against someone, a neighbour encroaching on land, someone making too much noise or creating smells, an official complaint can be made. It is called a *denuncia* meaning to report or to declare and is made to the *Guardia Civil*. The form, called the *Certificate de Denuncia*, is completed with an official stamp. It may take time, but each complaint will be investigated by the police and in most cases, the matter ends there. *Denuncias* can also be made by phone in Spanish and English by calling 902 102 112 and on the internet in Spanish at www.policia.es.

In the event of theft or loss of property a police report is required within 24 hours in order to reclaim this loss from an insurance company. The report is again a *denuncia*. In large cities and tourist areas where theft is common or pickpockets operate, it seems to be a policy to have a translator on hand at police station to offer help.

A *denuncia* is not the same as bringing charges to a court. Going to court to present a formal charge is more serious where the offending person and the person making the accusation must appear in front of a judge who will hear the case.

If a passport is lost or has been stolen (a common occurrence), and you need to travel home immediately, it is possible to obtain an emergency passport, valid for a one-way trip only, from the nearest British Consulate. To do this it is necessary to present a Lost and Stolen passport form, a passport application form, a *denuncia* and two passport-sized photographs. It is possible to wait at the consulate for an application to be processed, or to apply for a replacement passport from the British Consulate-General in Madrid by post.

GOING TO COURT

Too slow! Too costly! Too formal! However it is unlikely that the average citizen of Spain will have anything to do with a court. Spanish courts do work well, albeit slowly. The role of an Examining Magistrate has been well publicised on television whenever a high profile UK citizen is arrested. A starting point for any private action is to consult an *abogado* who will advise a correct course of action, the chance of success and costs involved.

Having said that, it is possible to go it alone. The Law of Civil Judgment makes it easier for businesses and services to pursue a case for bad debts allowing a claim to be filed without a lawyer for debts up to 30,000€. Once the facts are presented the judge will order a hearing. If the debtor does not appear, of if the judge decides they have not presented a valid reason for not paying the debt, they will order the debtor to pay up within 20 days. Further non-payment will result in the debtor's assets being seized by the court. The language barrier makes this a difficult procedure for the average foreigner, consequently hiring an *abogado* is necessary, which regrettably is precisely what this procedure is designed to avoid.

Legal aid

Going to court entails costs, mainly for pre-legal advice, solicitors' fees, publishing announcements in official journals and deposits required for lodging certain appeals and experts' fees. These costs normally have to be paid, up front, by the party concerned. At the end of the trial the court has to decide which party has to ultimately to bear the costs. This is governed by a principle of the loser paying.

Legal aid is a right for all members of the public who cannot afford the costs of a trial and have insufficient means, defined as where the total monthly income of the family unit is less than twice the national minimum wage set annually by the government. Even a non-resident may qualify for free legal aid.

Employees have the right to free representation before a labour court when they feel they have been mistreated by their Spanish employer. In this instance they must be in the social security system.

Legal aid is available for all cases involving sums of over 900€ and covers proceedings, appeals and enforcement of judgments. In cases involving smaller sums, for which the services of a solicitor and barrister are not compulsory, legal aid may be granted where the other party does have legal representation, or when explicitly called for by the judge or court to ensure the two parties are on an equal footing.

An application form for legal aid is available from Legal Guidance Departments of Bar Associations (*Colegios de Abogados*), or the Offices of Senior Judges (*Decanatos*) at courts and at provincial Legal Aid Commissions. The request should include documentation showing personal financial circumstances, the financial situation of the members of the family unit, the legal protection sought and particulars of the litigants.

As a rule, the solicitor (*abogado*) is appointed by the Bar Association on a rota. However, the individual may choose a solicitor, provided they agree not to charge. The legal professional who actually appears in court has to be someone other than the *abogado*. This is a barrister (*procurador*) who represents clients in court throughout the trial.

JUDICIAL STRUCTURE

Juzgados de Paz (Justices of the Peace)

These courts are now becoming obsolete, only operating in small communities which have no other courts. They are presided over by a single lay Justice appointed on an honorary basis by the Provincial Court and only hear minor civil cases.

Juzgados de Primera Instancia e Instruccion (Courts of the First Instance and Instruction)

This is the most common form of court found in all towns with a population of more than 20,000. It is divided into two parts. Courts of the First Instance are concerned with civil and commercial cases and supervising the work of Civil Registrars. Courts of Instruction act as Examining Magistrates investigating and preparing criminal cases to be tried in other courts. They may also try minor cases, where the maximum penalty does not exceed 30 days' imprisonment, and hear appeals against judgments handed down by Justices of the Peace.

This is the first step on the judicial ladder where an action can be brought to recover unpaid debts such as failure to pay the rent, or claims for damages following an assault, or a breach of contract such as poor building standards. An *abogado* is required. In some cases an expert witness, *perito judicial*, is also required to give a professional view on a subject.

While the majority of legal actions will start and finish at the Courts of First Instance, any appeal will lead to a higher level court such as the *Audiencia Provincial* and then ultimately to the *Tribunal Supremo*, the highest court of all.

Juzgados de lo Penal (Criminal Courts)

Presided over by a single professional judge, they hear cases where the maximum penalty prescribed by law does not exceed six years' imprisonment.

Audiencia Provincial (Provincial Court)

There is one in each province and they are presided over by a panel of three professional judges. Named after the province, its jurisdiction extends throughout that province. They try all criminal cases where the prescribed sentence could exceed six years' imprisonment and hear appeals against sentences by the lower courts.

Audiencia Nacional (National Court)

They are constituted as the Provincial Courts with National jurisdiction. The court tries all cases involving crimes, including major drug trafficking and monetary offences which are deemed to have been committed against the State and may attract a sentence of over six years' imprisonment. It also decides on extradition requests and hears appeals against sentences by the lower central courts.

Tribunal Supremo (Supreme Court)

The Supreme Court is the highest level of justice in the Spanish system. It is divided into five Chambers (Civil, Criminal, Labour, Military and Public Affairs) and hears appeals for the annulment, or revision, of sentences handed down by the National or Regional High Courts. It would also try civil or criminal cases against the President of the Government, Ministers and Members of Parliament, etc.

Other courts

While the centrepiece of the judicial system is *Juzgados de Primera Instancia e Instruccion* (Courts of the First Instance and Instruction), together with a tiered approach depending on seriousness and appeals, there are a number of other courts for specific subjects such as work related issues, prisons, minors and constitutional matters. Details are given below.

Juzgados de Menores (Minors' Courts)

Presided over by a single professional judge they hear all cases, including criminal charges, involving minors under the age of 16.

Juzgados de lo Social (Labour Courts)

Presided over by a single professional judge they hear all labour and work-related cases.

Juzgados de Vigilancia Penitenciaria (Courts of Prison Vigilance)

They provide judges who look after the operation of prisons and the legal rights of detainees. They are responsible for granting parole and any conditions attached to it.

Juzgados Centrales de Instruccion (Central Instruction Courts)

They act as examining magistrates investigating and preparing cases to be tried in either the Central Criminal Courts or the National Court.

Juzgados Centrales de lo Penal (Central Criminal Courts)

Located only in Madrid, they are presided over by a single professional judge. They hear cases involving crimes against the state which are punishable by less than six years' imprisonment.

Tribunal Constitucional (Constitutional Court)

This limits itself to considering constitutional matters and cases in which it is alleged constitutional rights have been infringed.

Tribunal Superior de Justicia de las Comunidades Autonomas
(Regional High Courts)

Each Autonomous Community also has one of these courts. They have no direct involvement in criminal cases unless these infringe the privileges and immunities of local government officials or the judiciary. They are generally involved in commercial disputes and litigation against public sector bodies.

ACCIDENTS AND ASSAULTS

There are two methods for claiming damages: through criminal or civil proceedings. Reports must be made within two months of the accident or assault if criminal proceedings are to be taken. For civil proceedings, reports must be lodged within one year of the incident.

The examining magistrate decides if further action is to be taken, and it is their sole decision to order an arrest or further investigation. The magistrate will summon witnesses as necessary. Their costs should be recoverable, but reimbursements are usually less than expected. It can take up to two years or longer for a case to be brought to trial.

Injured parties may engage private lawyers to help prosecute their case and look after their interests in court. There is no provision for this expenditure to be reimbursed other than as part of a general judgment on costs which would then depend on the accuser's ability to pay.

Applications for compensation are made to the court within whose jurisdiction the incident took place. In cases involving physical injury, an examination by the court's doctor will be necessary. The examining magistrate decides whether compensation is payable by the defendant and how much it should be. The Criminal Compensation Fund Law became effective in 1996, and provides for compensation in cases of death, serious injury, serious damage to mental health or sexual abuse.

IF YOU ARE ARRESTED

An offence normally first comes to the notice of the police when the injured party makes a report or complaint (*denuncia*) or when the police are called to the scene of a reported crime. However, in some instances such as a result of enquiries or traffic offences, the police themselves make the initial complaint. The police are obliged to report the arrest of any British Citizen to the nearest Consulate immediately, where every effort will be made for a consular officer to visit the detainee within 72 hours of arrest.

Upon arrest a person should be informed of the charges against them. He or she is then likely to be held temporarily in a police cell until a formal statement answering the charges can be taken. After this, but in any event within 72 hours of arrest, the accused will be brought before an examining magistrate or released. A lawyer and if necessary an interpreter must be present when the statement is taken and when the accused appears before the judge. If the accused is unable to pay for, or unwilling to appoint, a lawyer, one will be assigned to him or her at no charge from a duty roster of the Bar Association (*Colegio de Abogados*). It is important to note that a lawyer is present solely to ensure that the accused's rights are not violated and that the correct legal procedures are followed. They are not there to 'defend' the prisoner.

The examining magistrate

When appearing before the examining magistrate the accused will be asked to confirm or deny the statement previously made to the police or to make a further statement. This initial appearance is not a hearing on the merits of the case. Rather, it is a brief oral examination by the judge of the accused and will normally be based on evidence submitted by the police. From this they will determine whether there is a case to answer and, if so, decide whether the accused should be released without charges, placed on provisional liberty with or without bail, or committed to prison pending further investigation. The decision by the examining magistrate is subject to appeal by both the defendant and the prosecutor.

The examining magistrate is in charge of investigating the crime, its circumstances, perpetrators and any other matters relating to the offence. They are assisted in this by the judicial police (members of the national police force assigned to their office). The State Prosecutor or defence lawyer may ask the examining magistrate to follow specific leads in the investigation. When the investigation is completed it is the prosecutor who lays the formal accusation based on the evidence to the court. During the investigation stage all evidence, including police documents and witnesses' statements, are reserved documents. Copies will not normally be released to interested parties or their representatives although, of course, defence lawyers and, if appointed, private prosecuting lawyers do have the right of access and examination.

On receipt of the examining magistrate's committal proceedings the trial court will pass it first to the Public Prosecutor's Office and, if one has been appointed, to the private lawyer assisting in the prosecution. They must then submit their provisional written observations on the case and their recommendations on sentencing to the court. These, with the original proceedings, are passed to the defence lawyer who must, usually within 15 days, provide the court with their own written observations. Only after these have been considered will a trial date be set. If the accused has not already engaged a lawyer they will continue to be represented by their first state lawyer throughout the proceedings.

Appeals

A sentence from the criminal courts can be appealed to a higher court by either the defence or the prosecution. Any such appeal must be filed within five days of the judgment. Decisions by a Supreme Court are final. Only if it is asserted that a Constitutional right has been violated can an appeal be lodged with the Constitutional Court. Should new evidence come to light after a person has been sentenced there is provision for the original judgment to be reviewed.

Prison

The Spanish prison authorities require written consent from a foreign prisoner to inform a Consular representative of an arrest and continued detention. The British Consul's role is to protect a prisoner's basic rights. Refusal to have the Consul informed could impede such a protective role, which includes taking up any serious complaint with the prison administration, informing next-of-kin of the situation, helping relatives with prison visits and transfers of funds whilst in prison.

A Consular officer will regularly visit all British prisoners. This would normally be as soon as possible after being notified of first arrest, once every three months for remand prisoners and at least once a year thereafter. Consuls cannot:

• give legal advice;

• investigate a crime;

• instigate court proceedings;

- get better treatment for a British national than is provided for locals or other nationals;

- or intervene in the Spanish judicial process to obtain the release of a British prisoner.

Under the provisions of the Council of Europe Convention on the Transfer of Sentenced Persons, a British prisoner in Spain may apply to serve the remainder of their sentence in the United Kingdom. To be eligible for such a transfer the sentence should be final with no other charges outstanding.

Footballers abroad

A heady mix of professional footballers and allegations of sexual assault made the headlines in 2004. It demonstrated to the UK public a Spanish legal system different from their own, where an examining magistrate and not the police is the key figure. This summary has been compiled with assistance from newspapers at the time but names have been omitted.

Background

La Manga Club is a favourite destination for English football clubs, offering a balmy setting for a winter break and providing coaches with state-of-the-art training facilities to help keep the players focused. The 1,400-acre luxury complex, set within olive and lemon groves, boasts international-standard football pitches, three 18-hole championship golf courses, a tennis centre, spa, gym and beaches fringed with palm trees. At the heart of the resort is a five-star hotel, surrounded by landscaped gardens, fountains and a luxurious swimming pool.

Report of Thursday 4 March 2004

Eight footballers were held overnight in Spanish custody over allegations of sexual assault by three women in the resort of La Manga. The players were on a five-day training break when arrested on Wednesday evening after three German women made a complaint to Spanish police. They were questioned in a closed court in Cartagena the next day and two were released. The other six players will remain in custody tonight. They have not been charged with anything. A judge will be considering their cases tomorrow (Friday).

A spokesman for the Spanish Interior Ministry said: 'Accusations have been made involving rape. Three women alleged that the players forced their way into a hotel room in La Manga early on Monday where some of the men sexually assaulted them.'

Report of Saturday 6 March 2004

Three footballers face months in a Spanish jail before standing trial for sexual assaults on three women. The players were on suicide watch last night in the hospital wing of Sangonera jail in Spain. At the hearing a fourth player was released on bail and charges against a further two were dropped.

The jailed trio are being held under 'sexual aggression' laws, which in the Spanish legal system can range from groping to rape. Spanish newspapers now report that the women involved are black Kenyans, resident in Germany.

At a hearing yesterday, a Spanish judge remanded all three of the footballers in custody. The trio, who strongly protest their innocence, could face jail sentences of up to 12 years if found guilty. The three women were questioned by Judge Pilar Perez Martin, a woman examining magistrate.

Report of Wednesday 17 March 2004

Sangonera La Verde prison in Murcia, southern Spain, one week, St Mary's Stadium in Southampton for a reserve-team fixture the next. Such is life for the 'La Manga Three' the latest high-profile casualties in a sport that at times appears bent on self-destruction.

Thirteen days ago at the luxury La Manga resort, which the players had visited for warm weather training, things turned nasty. Eight players were initially implicated in an alleged incident involving three women. Three were eventually charged with 'sexual aggression'.

Shame and ignominy has been heaped upon them even after they were bailed for the collective sum of about £200,000. Last night they received an unsympathetic response from the crowd. For the three the possibility of a trial remains. Only in the fullness of time will it be revealed if it was saints or sinners playing at St Mary's last night.

Report of Friday 16 April 2004

Speculation exists that three footballers accused of sexually assaulting three women at their hotel will have to stand trial in Spain. The law states they will face a professional jury of three judges over the rape allegations. The examining magistrate who has been investigating the case is to make an official announcement today.

When she did, the charges were DROPPED.

FURTHER READING

Paul Preston, *Juan Carlos – A People's King*. London: Harper Collins. A lesson in how someone works hard to be head of state in a modern democracy.

3
Who am I ...
Where am I Going?

INTRODUCTION

Unsurprisingly, documents required for an EU citizen staying in Spain are different from those for a non-EU citizen. Then there is the length of stay – tourist or permanent. Some people live permanently in Spain but never take out a *Residencia*. They are illegally living in a country where there are clear benefits in obeying rules to become a legal resident. Domiciliation, a UK law, and citizenship are separate issues which are also explored in this chapter.

EUROPEAN UNION CITIZENS

Tourist status

The EU allows free movement in its member states for all its citizens, provided they have a national identity card or a passport. The UK is one of the few countries in Europe which does not issue an ID card but this is proposed to change. Until then a valid passport is required for UK citizens to enter Spain and for internal identification purposes thereafter.

A person on a short-term stay is classed as a tourist and can enter Spain for a period of up to 90 days with:

- a passport (the only legal requirement);

- form E111 for temporary reciprocal medical cover;

- a driving licence;

- some Euros;

- a credit card; since the introduction of the Euro virtually all Bureaux de Change have disappeared, but ATMs (cash dispenser machines) take all international cards with instructions in English.

A further 90-day extension, called a *permanencia*, can be obtained once per calendar year, so with this extension it is possible to stay as a 'tourist' for a total of six months. To apply for a *permanencia,* which is stamped in the passport, go to the foreigners' department of the nearest police station with a passport, two photos, and some evidence of your ability to finance a stay in Spain for a further 90 days. The *permanencia* is a little used procedure, but it technically bridges the gap between a 90-day short-term stay and permanent residence over 180 days. A tourist is a person who spends less than six months in Spain in one calendar year. A tourist may own a home and many do! Anyone who stays more than six months must apply for a *Residencia.*

Fiscal identification number

All residents or non-residents with financial dealings in Spain must have an identification number. It is called *Numero Identification de Extranjero (NIE)*, the significant word *Extranjero* meaning foreigner. *Numero de Identification Fiscal (NIF)* is the equivalent for Spaniards, which in their case also serves as an identity and passport number.

To get an *NIE* go to the foreigners' department of a police station with a passport and one copy, two photographs and complete the relevant form provided. Foreigners will quickly become accustomed to a way of life dependent on personal identification by an *NIE* number. An *NIE* is required for:

- purchase of a property, a car and other expensive items;

- dealing with the tax authorities;

- identification on other documents such as insurance policies or bank records.

Permanent status

Intending to live permanently or to spend more than six months each year in Spain? Then no later than 90 days after arriving, begin the process of applying for a *Residencia* (this is effectively an identity card). To do this, again visit the foreigners' department at the police station with the following documents:

- copy of a valid passport and *NIE* number;

- three passport-sized colour photographs;

- the completed form.

At the police station finger prints are taken and in about six months a plastic *Residencia* card is issued. It's your new identity in Spain and renewable every five years. The passport goes into the file at home to be used for international travelling. Obtaining a *Residencia* also necessitates a visit to the bank to change personal details and account numbers. It also means paying income tax to Spain rather than to a 'home' country.

Someone entering Spain as a student or as a tourist, and then taking up employment or self-employment, should read Chapter 13 Working in Spain, where details of a combined work permit/*residencia* application are outlined. A person entering Spain as a potential employer should still obtain a *residencia*.

Who does not require a *residencia*?

EU dependants of an EU or Spanish national, or pensioners who have worked in Spain and receive their pension from the Spanish social security system, do not need to hold a residence card, and can also live in Spain with a valid passport.

Other documents

When moving to Spain permanently it is wise to have the following documents available.

- Birth and marriage certificates.

- Credit facilities to open a new bank account if seeking a business account.

- CVs translated into Spanish, if seeking employment. Pre-approved work permits are no longer required for EU nationals.

- Vehicle documents, if temporarily driving a car registered outside Spain.

- If a UK pensioner, form E121 obtained from The Pension Service, Newcastle upon Tyne, which shows the pensioner has been in the UK National Health system and is entitled to entry into the Spanish health system. An E form means European, demonstrating a uniformity of approach within the EU.

The Hague Apostille

Some documents need to be certified as true. A Certificate of Apostille is an internationally recognised form on which an authority in one country validates a document to another country. A stamp is attached called an *apostille* (a Spanish word meaning note) certifying the document is legal. This is done in the UK. In Spain it is then translated into Spanish by a 'legal translator'. Documents issued in the UK which need to have the *apostille* attached for use in Spain are covered by the 1961 Hague Convention. Spain became a signatory in 1978. Examples would be birth and marriage certificates, but educational documents no longer need an *apostille*. Any Consular office in Spain can arrange British documents which need an *apostille*. Alternatively sent directly to: Legislation Office, Foreign and Commonwealth Office, Old Admiralty Building, The Mall, London SW1A 2LG.

NON-EUROPEAN UNION CITIZENS

Things are more complicated for non-EU residents. Non-EU foreigners need a visa to enter Spain, except if an agreement exists between Spain and the foreigner's home country to enter on a normal tourist basis, which is the normal situation. Application for a visa is made to a Spanish Consulate located in the home country before leaving. Visas are handled by the Spanish Ministry of Foreign Affairs through its consulate abroad.

There are different types of visas. They are issued according to the purpose for entering Spain: studying, working, tourism, investment, etc. An application should be made according to individual needs. It is not possible to enter Spain on a tourist visa and then apply to stay as something else without returning home to obtain the appropriate visa. In general terms three types of visas exist:

- **Transit visa**. This is given to individuals or groups of foreigners passing through Spanish ports or airports without entering Spanish territory. This visa also allows foreigners to pass through Spanish territory for a maximum of five days.

- **Temporary stay visa**. This is issued for foreigners who wish to stay in Spain for up to three months within a six-month time period. There are different categories such as group visas for short stays, visas for diplomatic personnel or similar and visas to study in Spain.

- **Residence visa**. This should not be confused with the residence permit, which is also necessary in most cases. This is initially granted for one year, and it may be renewed for an additional two-year period, once it has expired. It is also possible to apply for a permanent residency visa, which must be renewed every five years. There are three specific categories:

1 For reuniting a family. It could be given to the spouse provided that the marriage is valid; or to the descendants provided that they are not married and are under 18 years of age.

2 For working in Spain when the foreigner needs a work permit; when professionals or scientists are hired by a Spanish university or the Spanish government.

3 For asylum. This is issued to foreigners with refugee status.

A visa is stamped in the passport. Documentary evidence to obtain a visa is stringent and depends on the reason for entry. Proof of financial resources, pre-arranged medical health cover and no criminal record are basic requirements. A reference, an employment contract, or proof of admission to a Spanish educational establishment, or a letter from a family if an au pair, are additional requirements. Except for some professional occupations a work permit, secured by a prospective employer from the *Delagacion Provincial del Ministerio de Trabajo*, is also required. A Consulate will judge each case separately but the key is sufficient means of financial support within Spain.

Once a visa is obtained it is relatively straightforward to obtain a *Residencia*. This requires a letter showing registration with the Spanish Consulate back home, passport and copies, photos, marriage and birth certificates, a statement from a Spanish bank showing proof of financial means and lastly the completed form with an appropriate fee.

The majority of non-EU citizens entering Spain, legally or illegally, are Moroccans. However non-EU also means Swiss, American, Canadian and people from the Southern Hemisphere including those from Spain's former colonies. While entering Spain may be more difficult for those with non-EU status, regrettably separate identification due to place of origin continues to rear its head once in Spain – see Chapter 15 On the Road.

TOURIST OR RESIDENT?

It is well known that the British population, and for that matter foreigners from Northern Europe living in various Mediterranean locations, are not clearly defined by their own social perception of tourist, seasonal resident, temporary resident or permanent resident. The law is quite clear irrespective of property ownership and taxation. For up to six months' stay a person is a non-resident. For over six months' stay a person is a resident. Spain has a problem with illegal Moroccan immigrants but many Northern Europeans live permanently in Spain without a *Residencia* and without paying taxes – they too are illegal immigrants with only their passports protecting them from greater legal penalties. Why do they do it?

Perhaps the answer lies in a reluctance to grapple with red tape in changing status, or perhaps they are reluctant to break the ties with home. Are they seeking to vanish from various authorities or hoping to escape taxation? Are they ignorant of the facts? There are no benefits in maintaining a tourist status if you are resident more than 183 days in Spain – only the risk of a fine.

A person who lives in Spain for more than 183 days, whether or not holding a *Residencia*, becomes liable to pay Spanish income tax.

In fact the Spanish tax system is geared to provide greater tax relief to residents than to non-residents by reducing capital gains tax, not having five per cent of the price withheld when selling a property pending a review of capital gains liabilities, and a reduction in inheritance tax, *renta* tax and income tax. (See Chapter 14 on Understanding Personal Taxation and Chapter 17 on Wills and Inheritance Tax.)

DOMICILE

Where a person is domiciled is a feature of UK law. Only UK law! An individual's domicile is not necessarily the same as either their country of residence or nationality. Domicile is a totally different matter. The basic rule is a person is domiciled in the country in which they have their home permanently or indefinitely. This is often described as the country which the person regards as their 'homeland', and frequently as the place where a person intends to die. A place of domicile does not have to be the country in which a person has the closest personal association. A person can live in a country for many years and still remain domiciled elsewhere. It's a little bit confusing.

Domicile of origin

At birth, an individual acquires a domicile of origin which is the same as the father's domicile at the time of the child's birth. This is not necessarily the same as the country in which the child was born. It is possible for someone to have a domicile of origin in a country which they have never visited. The domicile of origin never changes and it revives automatically if there is any doubt about an individual's 'domicile of choice'.

Domicile of choice

The domicile of origin can be altered to become another country; this is called the 'domicile of choice'. This change is not easy as there is a strong tendency to favour retention of the domicile of origin. Furthermore, if a person loses a domicile of choice, by leaving an adopted country and moving to a third country, they are likely to reacquire their domicile of origin. There are two main elements for a domicile of choice to replace a domicile of origin:

* First, the individual must be physically present in the new country and be a tax resident.

* Second, they must intend to reside permanently in the new country.

But for most people permanently retiring to Spain, taking out a *Residencia* and paying tax to Spain, it is normal to assume they will continue to retain UK domicile status. In other words the individual is not domiciled in Spain. Equally a person visiting Spain for a few months each year, owning a holiday home and paying tax to the UK, is domiciled in the UK. This slightly unusual position is readily accepted by authorities in both countries, giving a basis for planning inheritance tax.

While the domiciliation of a person retiring to Spain is clear, this is not the situation with a wealthy person, still earning, living in Spain and paying income tax to Spain (in other words, a tax exile). Unless they can prove otherwise, they are domiciled in Spain. There are a number of ways in which domicile status can be satisfactorily tested but in practice the Inland Revenue will not consider this until it becomes relevant for some tax purpose. A wealthy individual in this position should consider if it is more advantageous to retain UK domicile and face UK inheritance tax liabilities or pay income tax and become liable for death duties in Spain.

NATIONALITY

If a person moves to Spain, takes out a *Residencia*, earns a salary, pays taxes in Spain, marries a Spaniard and raises a family it still does not make them a Spaniard. They remain British, or Irish, or whatever their passport states, until they choose to formally renounce their nationality in order to become Spanish.

Some countries permit dual nationality and do not mind if one of their citizens takes on another nationality. A British citizen, for example, can take another nationality without renouncing their British citizenship, but Spain does not recognise dual nationality. Therefore British citizens who take Spanish nationality are regarded by the British as British and Spanish, and by the Spanish as solely Spanish. Marriage to a foreigner does not change the nationality of a partner. A British person who marries a Spaniard remains British unless they apply for Spanish nationality.

The basic requirement for applying for Spanish nationality is a residence period in Spain of ten years although this is substantially reduced in the case of marriage. The paperwork required comprises birth certificate, parents' birth certificates, marriage certificate, all authenticated by the Consulate and translated into Spanish by official translators, plus proof of holding a *Residencia* for ten years.

A new citizen to Spain will be required to renounce a former nationality, swear an oath of allegiance to the Spanish Crown. If they are wise they will make out a last will and testament according to Spanish law.

ESTADO CIVIL

The Family Book is a document of great importance to Spaniards. So too is a person's civil state (*Estado Civil*). Together, this is a full set of information about a person required by various legal authorities, particularly a notary dealing with wills and property purchase, and civil authorities dealing with births, marriage and deaths. They will ask for full name and address; occupation; nationality and passport number; maiden name; names of parents; date and place of birth; date and place of marriage and if appropriate date and place of divorce. Authorities are entitled to ask for proof and some may require an official translation of certificates into Spanish, but often an official will accept a verbal confirmation. The notary dealing with public documents will treat an *Estado Civil* with reverence.

There is also the issue of matrimonial 'regime' (*regimen matrimonial*), something that has to be specified in Spain when you marry as it will apply to the relationship. No such arrangement applies in the UK. There are two options:

- a regime of common ownership of assets (*comunidad de bienes*) where all assets acquired after the marriage belong to both;

- or a regime of separate ownership of assets (*separacion de bienes*) where each spouse is entitled to own assets in their own name, upon which the other spouse has no automatic claim.

If a comparison has to be made, then marriage under UK law is the second option. If asked in Spain for a matrimonial regime simply state that no formal regime exists but it is similar to *separacion de bienes*.

MOVING HOUSEHOLD EFFECTS

All import duties have been abolished on the movement of household goods within the EU.

European removal companies are sound professional organisations normally belonging to the International Federation of Furniture Removers. They have well-established procedures both operationally and administratively. The paperwork is best left to them.

It is wise to leave TV sets at home as the Spanish sound system and receiving frequency differs from other European countries. Washing machines work successfully but the plumbing of a Spanish home does not allow for a hot water fill. Computers, vacuum cleaners and other domestic items all operate successfully on Spanish voltages.

For non-EU nationals the movement of household goods, but not cars, is free, but the procedure is tortuous. In this case the Spanish government grants a privilege of importing household effects and personal possessions free of customs duty. It is not necessary to purchase property in order to justify this, but holding a *Residencia* is, and regrettably a deposit of approximately 50 per cent of the value of the goods must be made, which is returned within one year. Conditions relating to this privilege are that a person has not been a resident in Spain during the two years prior to the importation of the goods; that the goods enter the country within three months of the person's own arrival in Spain; that the goods are at least six months old, and not sold for a further two years. The starting point for this procedure is the Spanish Consulate in the home country ... and of course a form.

DEALING WITH PETS

There is absolutely no reason why a pet cannot enter Spain, or for that matter travel through an intermediate country such as France. The United Kingdom has recently relaxed quarantine regulations, bringing its approach more in line with other European countries. It may be necessary to travel to and from Spain frequently or unexpectedly, in which case any pet should have the necessary vaccinations, health checks and accompanying paperwork. The website of the Department of Environment www.defra.gov.uk/animalh/quarantine/index is useful.

The Pet Travel Scheme allows cats and dogs resident in the UK to visit certain other countries and return to the UK, without quarantine, provided that certain conditions are met thus eliminating the transmission of disease from country to country. Spain is one of the countries in the scheme. All cats and dogs must:

- be fitted with a microchip that meets an ISO specification so that it can be read by a standard microchip reader;

- be vaccinated against rabies with an approved vaccine and have booster vaccinations as recommended; pets must be at least three months old and be already fitted with a microchip before they can be vaccinated;

- be blood tested about 30 days after vaccination;

- wait at least six months after a successful blood test result before being allowed entry or re-entry into the UK.

Spain also requires an Export Health Certificate to allow a pet to enter the country. It is different from the PETS scheme. When in Spain have the pet fitted with a microchip which gives its new address.

Three documents are required to allow a pet to re-enter the UK:

- the PETS certificate certifying that the above conditions have been met before travel;

- an official Certificate of Treatment against a potentially dangerous type of tapeworm and ticks, which must be carried out by a vet between 24 to 48 hours before re-entering the UK;

- a Declaration of Residence to declare that a pet has not been outside any of the qualifying countries in the six months before entering the UK; this will be available from a transport company or from MAFF.

LETTING THE HOUSE BACK HOME

Some people, with the intention of living in Spain permanently, decide not to sell their old home to generate income. Let it out! It makes sense to put the letting of this property in the hands of experts. The Association of Residential Agents, formed in 1981, regulates letting agents and seeks to promote the provision of high standards of service to both landlords and tenants. Membership is restricted to those letting agents who can demonstrate good financial practices and have a good working knowledge of all the legal issues involved.

If the owner is classed as an overseas resident for tax purposes, the letting company is responsible for deducting income tax at base rate on the rental income, unless the Inland Revenue provides a tax exemption certificate.

AN EU IDENTITY CARD?

History of the *DNI*

The Spanish Identity Card, known to everyone as the *DNI* (*Documento Nacional de Identidad*) recently celebrated 60 years of existence. These cards were initiated on 2 March 1944 under General Franco's regime. The birth of the *DNI* was the result of chaos caused by the Spanish Civil War. Many citizens were either dead, missing or had emigrated. The War left the government not knowing the names of its people. Security letters issued by each of the previous warring faction were no longer valid. The 1944 decree would allow Franco's government to know who had survived.

Prisoners and those under police surveillance were the first to be obliged to carry the *DNI*, and then came men who, due to their profession or business, had to change their address regularly. Shortly after, all men in cities of over 100,000 were issued with *DNI*s and then those who lived in cities between 25,000 and 100,000 residents. In due course the *DNI* became compulsory for women who needed to travel due to their employment and then finally it reached the entire Spanish population.

In the early days, when not every area was covered by a National Police station, civil servants travelled from town to town to carry out the process, using donkeys to reach far flung rural and mountainous areas. A date was set with the mayor and everyone in the village would queue up with their photos and birth certificates – if any resident lacked such documents, then the local priest was called upon to verify an identity.

Naturally Franco had *DNI* card number 1, his wife number 2 and his daughter number 3, while the following six numbers were left unassigned in the event of more births within the Franco family. Card number 10 was assigned to King Juan Carlos and number 11 to Queen Sofia. Their eldest daughter, Cristina, has number 12 and so on.

The *DNI* today

Today every Spanish national is obliged to carry a *DNI*, which includes the bearer's signature, basic personal details and a reference to a national data bank in which everybody's fingerprints can also be found. Incorporated is the *Numero de Identificación Fiscal* (*NIF*) which as we have seen before is a fiscal, identity and passport number. Current *DNI* cards must be renewed every ten years and despite the inconvenience everyone recognises a need for some form of personal identification. In fact 60 years on, it is now an accepted way of life to have a *DNI*.

Surprising as it may seem, until 1962 the *DNI* was also given to all foreign residents in Spain but now their details are incorporated in a *Residencia* which also includes the *Numero Identificación de Extranjero* (*NIE*) and is valid for five years.

Over the years the *DNI* card design has changed many times. The first design had green borders and the imperial eagle stamp – a symbol of the Franco government – in the top right-hand corner. Information typed on the card included, apart from the usual personal details (name, address, parents' name, sex, date and place of birth), the person's social security affiliation and job. It gave the person a category according to his or her economic status – useful in post-war years.

Many modifications have since taken place in both content and presentation. A new digital *DNI* card has been issued from 2005 to include a microchip that will speed up all the necessary procedures a person is required to carry out with public administration offices and via the internet.

Spain is not the only country to have national ID cards as the majority of European countries issue them. This opens the door to a future EU ID card that will allow the members of the Union to travel freely on a common card.

SUMMARY

There are four classifications of people in Spain. These classifications start upon entry and govern life thereafter, e.g. employment, tax and motoring.

- EU nationals on a tourist visit;

- EU nationals who are resident (which includes Spaniards too);

- non-EU nationals on a tourist visit;

- non-EU nationals who are resident.

Issues of domiciliation and nationality, so favoured in the UK, are largely irrelevant in Spain.

FURTHER INFORMATION

Many publications on this subject are out of date. Some even mislead accidentally. Some from financial institutions mislead deliberately. However one website is worthy of mention: www.Spainlawyer.com

Blevins Franks give a lucid explanation on the complexities of UK domiciliation on www.blevinsfranks.com

Two books giving an additional social background to expatriate living are:

Karen Riley, *British on the Costa del Sol.* London: Taylor and Francis Books Ltd.

King, Warnes and Williams, *Sunset Lives.* Oxford: Berg.

4
Cash, Credit and Currency

INTRODUCTION

The Spanish banking system is as efficient as any in the world but, as one would expect, it has some different practices and procedures. Bank charges are high so care has to be exercised when transferring money across international boundaries. While there are no restrictions on the amount of money coming into or going out of Spain, it is monitored by the government. It is no longer possible to 'hide' interest payments in offshore accounts. Money laundering is tightly controlled in the UK but less so in Spain. It is not possible to obtain a 100 per cent mortgage on a property from a Spanish provider.

SPANISH BANKING

Banking in Spain is fragmented. There are about 150 different banks. They serve different markets and have different functions. Clearing banks, savings banks, lending banks, cooperative banks and some foreign banks of French, German or British parentage compete with each other. These banks have many branches but naturally some of the smaller outlets do not offer a full range of services.

The Spanish banking system has some unusual procedures but it is efficient, and usually staffed by friendly, hard working, multilingual people capable of offering a customer some of the most up-to-date services including telephone and internet banking. Credit or debit plastic cards are accepted for the purchase of consumer goods or for obtaining cash from an ATM (hole in the wall cash dispenser) of which there are many.

In selecting a Spanish bank it makes sense that some staff should speak English and that it has access to services such as mortgages and investments. It should be a main branch thus preventing delays in foreign transactions.

Bank accounts of residents and non-residents are distinguished from each other. A non-resident account is called *cuenta extranjera* and a cheque book (*talonario*) is marked *cuenta en euros de no residente*. Different tax regulations apply but the banking operation for a non-resident account is exactly the same as for a resident account.

A current account (*cuenta corriente*) pays a low rate of interest – practically nothing (0.1 per cent). A resident will have 15 per cent of interest earnings withheld and paid to the Spanish tax authorities – less than practically nothing – and a non-resident should declare any liability to the tax authorities back home. Yet this account will incur some of the highest bank charges in Europe irrespective of the currency involved. Write a cheque and a charge occurs; transfer a payment and a charge occurs. With the exception of some free banking, charges occur every time a transaction takes place. Spanish banking is expensive!

Deposit accounts exist. They pay different rates of interest depending on the amount invested, the time period fixed in advance and the currency in which they are held. Again a resident will have 15 per cent of the interest withheld by the bank to cover income tax. The bank gives a receipt and the amount is deducted from income tax liability upon completing an annual tax return.

Free banking

The use of a credit or debit card on motorway tolls is free of charge. So too is a cash withdrawal from an ATM on a debit card, provided it is within a bank's computerised system. There are two computer 'ring mains' in Spain – *Servis Red* and *Tele Banco*. All Spanish banks 'plug into' one or the other. It is not the brand of card that determines the charge, but the computer system completing the transaction. Using the wrong one attracts a charge of up to 2€ per transaction. No other transaction is free unless you are receiving a pension from the Spanish state system.

Al portador

Some tradesmen, among others, prefer a cheque (*talon*) made out to *al portador* (cash) as there is no record of who cashes it. It is a system of understating earnings for tax avoidance. Payment of services by this method usually 'forgets' *IVA* (VAT) from the charge so both parties benefit from the transaction. The use of personal cheques is less frequent in Spain than in most European countries. It is a country that prefers cash or credit cards. Post-dated cheques can be cashed immediately irrespective of the date and if a cheque is written with insufficient funds in the account, it is still possible to collect a partial amount up to the value of the available funds.

Bank statements

Anyone with a Spanish bank account will come across the practice of small, frequent statements. Monthly statements are not issued. After one or two transactions a statement is issued detailing any cash withdrawal, standing order or direct debit. A person with 12 normal transactions per month can expect four letters and probably ten to 14 slips of paper. A special account, for say a monthly mortgage payment, can expect two slips transferring money in and another two making the payment out. Do not be tempted to throw these slips away; in fact it is advisable to keep them all for at least two years as they are often the only receipt from a service provider. They are proof of payment for items such as car tax and are required for completion of an annual tax return (mortgage payments, bank fiscal statement and the payment of local taxes – *IBI*).

Letras

A *letra de cambio* is defined as a bill of exchange or a letter of credit (a written order directing a specified sum of money be paid to a specified person on a specified date) and is often used to make staged payments for a new house bought off plan. This peculiarly Spanish practice is used for staggered payments so a number of *letras* are made out for a purchased item. For example if a computer is purchased for 1200€ it may be paid by signing 12 *letras*, of 100€ each, one to be paid each month. The seller will make out the *letras* with amount, date, buyers' bank, etc and they will be signed by the purchaser. The seller will send each *letra*, on the due date, directly to purchasers' bank where it will be taken directly from the nominated account. Once signed, a *letra* is effectively cash. If the goods are faulty or if the *letras* are made out to the wrong person too bad! If a bank holds a *letra* then payment is expected irrespective of the circumstances. A custom exists of purchasing other people's *letras*. In the case of a builder for example, he will sell all the *letras* to a bank or other institution at a discount in return for immediate cash.

Domiciling a payment

In other countries it is simply called a direct debit. In Spain it is called *domiciliacion de pagos* or the domiciling of payments where the word domicile means home. It is used to pay electricity, water or local tax bills. It is useful for non-residents, who do not spend the whole year in Spain, ensuring services are not terminated for non-payment.

Savings tax directive

The EU's Directive on the taxation of savings income in the form of interest payments came into effect in 2005. EU Member States automatically exchange information on savings income, reporting all interest payments made. Luxembourg, Austria, Belgium, Switzerland, certain Caribbean territories as well as the Channel Islands and Isle of Man will, for a transitional period, levy a withholding tax on interest payments made to EU citizens. In the UK the Inland Revenue is reviewing people evading tax by using offshore bank accounts. A number of banks have already complied with the Revenue's request for cooperation.

TRANSFERRING MONEY

Regular transfers

The use of two accounts, one in the home country and one in Spain, should be enough for the transfer (*transferencia*) of money, pensions and day to day living expenses. The transfer of money between two accounts is straightforward irrespective of the currency involved but charges can vary and conversion from sterling or dollars into euros is expensive.

Some people prefer to use three accounts: a UK sterling account, a UK euro account and a Spanish euro account. They transfer sterling to euros in the UK, then transfer these euros to Spain with instructions that all transfer charges are to be allocated to the UK account. The advantages of this may not be immediately apparent, but the benefits are avoidance of Spanish bank charges and the full identification of currency transfer costs which is not possible with only two accounts.

Offshore banking has some advantages for investments and tax free savings. Since Gibraltar, an offshore centre, is so close to the Costa del Sol, it is still possible to bank offshore and live in Spain. Many offshore current accounts offer a cash or credit withdrawal worldwide. However charges of 2.25 per cent from the exchange rate and 1.5 per cent per withdrawal make offshore banking expensive. The benefits of offshore banking are now doubtful as the EU has closed tax avoidance loopholes by having an offshore bank declare any interest earned to the tax authorities of the account holder's country of residence.

Any time money is transferred from a UK bank to an account in Spain a charge occurs. There are some exceptions but try to avoid paying a sterling or dollar cheque into a Spanish bank account. The charges are high – around 0.55 per cent and there is a 14 to 21 day delay while a cheque clears. A cheque from another country in the euro zone suffers an even worse fate, taking six weeks to clear as there is no centralised clearing bank system. A normal cheque within Spain attracts a small charge but no delay.

To reduce bank charges always transfer money from outside Spain by electronic transfer. Always transfer euros, not sterling or dollars. Always use a rapid bank transfer system such as SWIFT which assures the money is sent quickly. The charge will be a fixed fee of around £20 and 0.25 per cent deducted from the official exchange rate from the UK bank and a further 0.25 per cent from the Spanish bank. This deduction, in total 0.5 per cent, can be paid by the sender or by the receiver, or split evenly which is the normal approach. European banks have introduced unique account numbers for all bank accounts, incorporating a code for the identity of the bank and branch involved as well as the account number of the individual customer.

These are known as IBAN numbers. This, not name, address, sort code and account number, should be quoted on all international currency transfers.

Specialist companies

Specialist companies, competing with UK banks, exist for the regular transfer of money abroad. A fixed monthly euro requirement will vary as the exchange rate varies, so it is not possible to be exactly sure how much sterling will be required to cover an overseas payment. Overseas payment plans allow the fixing of an exchange rate between sterling and euros for one year at a time. The monthly payments are collected from a UK bank by direct debit and transferred abroad on a set date each month. The costs of this service are an annual £50 fee and £7.50 per month, less than normal banking charges.

Large transfers

Transferring large amounts of money over a lengthy period of time from outside the euro zone requires careful consideration. The variable exchange rate has to be taken into account. At its launch the euro instantly revalued to 1.64€ against the pound but in the aftermath of 9/11 moved to 1.39€. Which currency is weak or strong is a matter of conjecture. Either way, this swing of 18 per cent is a major influence when large sums of money are transferred. It can take many months to purchase a property abroad, particularly in the case of a new development. It is therefore important to ensure protection from the volatility of exchange rates. This means that a property price quoted today is probably not the price eventually paid, especially in the event of staged payments when purchasing 'off plan'.

For example let us assume that you are UK resident buying a new villa in Spain. The developer will require a deposit in euros immediately, then further stage payments during construction over the next 18 months and a large payment upon completion. The price of the property is in euros and this will not increase unless the specification is upgraded.

The actual cost in sterling will be determined by the timing of the currency purchase. If the pound strengthens during construction the cost will decline, but if the euro strengthens costs will increase. To illustrate the potential volatility a property priced at 200,000€ would have cost £129,870 in January 2003 but increased by £12,980 to £142,850 by May (a ten per cent increase in just five months).

Strategies for currency fluctuation

One transfer strategy would be to buy all the euros now, thus fixing the cost at the outset. This is called buying currency for 'spot'. Deposit the bought currency to earn some interest and make payments to the developer as requested. Another transfer strategy would be to buy the euros each time they are required to be sent to the developer. This means the purchaser has no idea what the final cost of the property may be.

A more complex transfer strategy, but one that is gaining in popularity, is to buy a 'forward contract'. In essence, a forward contract means buying the currency now, and paying for it when there is a need to make the individual stage payments. The requirement is to pay ten per cent now and a 90 per cent balance upon the maturity of the contract. For example £50,000 worth of euros bought now but not sent for three months means agreeing the rate now, placing £5,000 on deposit, and paying the remaining £45,000 balance in three months. If the exchange rate moves in the three-month period this will not affect the situation as the currency was bought at the originally agreed rate. It is possible to fix a rate on all forward requirements up to 18 months.

A forward contract can therefore remove the risk of exposure to currency fluctuations, which can occur between the time of agreeing a purchase and the completion of a purchase of an overseas property. However if sterling strengthens, it is possible to end up with an inferior exchange rate, lower than that on the open market at any point in time, but that is a risk each individual must assess for themselves and offset against the stability of a forward contract.

FINANCIAL CONTROLS

Free movement of money

There are no regulations governing the movement of money to and from Spain, but the Spanish government do like to know what is happening. As a consequence they have developed a reporting system by which most transactions involving foreign exchange (*divisas*) is recorded. This declaration does not mean authorities deny the transfer, only that it is reported. Banks record this information with their customers not realising it is taking place. 'What is reason for the transfer?' asks the international clerk at a UK bank when setting up a monthly direct transfer. 'What is the bill of exchange for?' asks the manager at a Spanish bank when a large sum is withdrawn to pay for a property. The payer, the receiver, the amount and reason for transfer are automatically identified.

The informality of these questions disguises a system administered by bank officials as an electronic transfer greater than 600€ should theoretically be reported. This applies to residents and non-residents alike. It refers to inward transactions and outward transactions. So in order to make a payment across national boundaries of more than 600€, the name and address of the recipient and the reason for the payment should be declared to the bank. Does this happen in practice? No! But it can happen in a selective way to individuals who may be suspected of money laundering.

Is it possible to carry a suitcase of money, cheques or gold bars into Spain? After all, there are virtually no cross-border or airport customs for EU citizens. Any amount under the value of 6,000€ is completely unregulated. Any amount greater than 6,000€ should be declared to customs authorities when entering Spain. Taking out of Spain more than 6,000€ but less than 30,000€ should be recorded on a form available at the bank when the cash is obtained and presented to the customs at the point of departure. Taking out a sum greater than 30,000€ must be accompanied by a form and permission from the *Direccion General de Transacciones Exteriores*, which is normally granted. As stated previously, the government does not wish to restrict the movement of cash, merely to know what is happening.

Falsification of any of the information on a form is a legal offence. Authorisation to export money does not fit with the EU Directive on the free circulation of money. The European High Court has ruled that Spain may require notification but cannot limit the amount taken out. Spain therefore maintains a check on the amounts of foreign exchange passing across its borders and keeps an eye on an individual's tax obligations. But the bottom line is, any amount of funds can be transferred in any choice of currency – just fill in a form.

Money laundering

The UK's Money Laundering Regulations came into effect in 2004. This new legislation, coupled with amendments to the Proceeds of Crime Act 2002, creates a new code of statutory responsibility for all financial and legal professionals based in the UK to report any suspicion of tax evasion to the Inland Revenue, wherever in the world the offence may have occurred. Where a UK regulated financial or legal adviser has clients who live abroad, the adviser will report the suspicion to the authorities who, in turn, will relay this information to the tax authority of the country of residence of the individual. Money laundering is widely defined and includes tax evasion. Where criminal conduct occurs outside the UK it is still within the scope of the Act and constitutes an offence as if it had occurred in the UK.

Financial advisors, solicitors, accountants and estate agencies are obliged to report to the authorities any suspicions they have that a client may have deliberately failed to declare all their income on their tax return. They are prohibited from informing the client about the report. Failure to report transgressions, or even just suspicions if there are reasonable grounds, will result in professional organisations being penalised by fines or imprisonment. The obligation to report will override the duty of confidentiality owed to a client.

However this is a UK law and does not embrace similar companies or laws in Spain.

Certificate of Non-Residence

A transaction to buy a Spanish property can be completed outside Spain, for example money transferred from a buyer's account in Edinburgh to a seller's account in Dublin. But to do this a Certificate of Non-Residence is required. It is issued in Spain by the Ministry of the Interior and again helps the Spanish tax man keep track of where the money comes from and goes to. This will take time; but without it a notary will not approve a property purchase.

MORTGAGES AND LOANS

A resident can borrow freely from outside Spain in any foreign currency for sums up to 1.5€ million without any authorisation provided the lender is not based in a 'tax haven'. A home-buyer in Spain can therefore obtain a mortgage from a lending institution in any country and in any currency denomination. In practice it is different. Lenders are always reluctant to lend against a property located in another country for it is difficult to repossess a foreign property if anything goes wrong.

However, lenders in Britain are quite relaxed about a homeowner's equity in their UK homes being used to fund the purchase of a second property overseas. Most people who are looking to buy overseas have a lot of equity. As long as the repayments are affordable, extending a UK mortgage should not be a problem. In the majority of cases a UK mortgage will be in the same currency as the borrower is earning. It is easier to arrange than an overseas mortgage and the costs of remortgaging in the UK will be less than those involved in arranging an overseas mortgage.

The Spanish banks too can be mortgage providers. Charges on a euro-denominated mortgage are calculated on a different basis to those on a UK sterling-denominated mortgage. Spanish mortgage rates are commonly quoted as Euribor plus a percentage. So for example a mortgage advertisement will state 'Euribor + 1 per cent'. Euribor is the Interbank lending rate used across the entire euro zone. As such, it is used as a common benchmark for consumer borrowing across a wide range of loans including credit cards and mortgages.

The Spanish mortgage market

There are no building societies or their equivalent in Spain with the exception of a few of UK parentage. Spanish banks therefore have a captive market for the provision of home finance. Spanish mortgages are on a repayment basis with loan and interest both repaid by instalments. Endowment and interest-only mortgages are not known in Spain. The criteria for granting a Spanish mortgage are similar, but more restrictive than in the UK.

- The earnings of one or both purchasers are taken into account. Allowances are made for letting income.

- The property is valued not at market value, but at a rebuild cost per square metre. Most banks will not lend an amount whereby the monthly repayments are greater than 30 per cent of net disposable income.

- The maximum mortgage for a non-resident is around 60 per cent of the valuation and for a resident around 80 per cent.

- A combination of a low valuation based on rebuilding cost and a low mortgage based on that valuation means an actual mortgage can be as low as 40 per cent of the market value of the property.

- Mortgages are usually granted for a maximum of 15 years and repaid before age 75.

- A separate mortgage deed does not exist. The existence of a mortgage is stated in the *escritura* prepared by the *notario*.

- The cost of a new mortgage is around five per cent and one per cent for redemption. Life insurance for the amount borrowed is also required.

- When buying off plan with stage payments a mortgage will only be granted at final payment, in the presence of the *notario*, which means the size of the mortgage is also limited to the size of the final payment. As this can be 60 per cent it is no problem. If the earlier stage payments are more substantial, banks will offer a credit facility for these payments.

If personal circumstances change, it may be necessary to raise money on a foreign property. The Spanish mortgage market is much less flexible than the UK's. Money is lent only in order to buy or improve a property. Once the property has been purchased, equity release is virtually impossible. So the only way to raise money on a foreign home is to sell it – and a forced sale is seldom on advantageous terms to the vendor.

However financing a property in Spain can offer more options than a straightforward mortgage extension on a UK home. Less risk is achieved by borrowing in euros. When currencies move, the asset will move in the same direction as the mortgage. Alternatively if income is in pounds, it is not a bad idea to have a loan in pounds as well, so any currency fluctuations will not change the payments.

Confused? Some people overcome this complexity by compromise, achieving a 100 per cent mortgage on a Spanish property, financing it by a 50 per cent mortgage extension on a UK property and a 50 per cent Spanish mortgage.

INVESTING IN SPAIN

It almost goes without saying that investments must only be made with a very good financial advisor, one who understands the taxation and investment regulations of Spain. Some financial advisors only offer advice in relation to their home country and write a disclaimer regarding the effect of their advice in Spain. This is of little help!

A variety of investments are available for the ex-pat in Spain. They are advertised in the weekly newspapers. In addition to conventional investments they range from dabbling in the futures market, buying up surrendered endowment policies and purchasing offshore unit trusts or bonds. Tempting these investments may be, but be warned that the 'independent financial advisor' is completely unregulated in Spain. Many such organisations simply sell financial products with little reference to a client's needs.

It is important to check both the financial advisor and the investment product. How long the company has actually been in business, qualifications of directors, their experience in financial markets and what commission they charge, are key questions, plus how you get the money back should it be necessary. Deals often appear to be too good to be true; they advertise returns of 15 per cent. Such investments may return a much higher percentage, but they are really only suited to those who can afford to take a risk.

One issue facing investors, who have lost considerable sums of money through high risk investments, is legal retribution. The investment company probably will not be registered in Spain and the Spanish legal system is poorly equipped to sue someone in Belize, Bermuda or even Bournemouth.

Contrast that with the Financial Services Authority in the UK which publishes a list of unauthorised firms that target investors. Strangely, the nearest equivalent publication in Spain comes from the British Consulate who gives details of the latest 'scams'.

Of course there is also tax to consider! It is clear that failure to disclose investment income is not a viable tax planning strategy. Information crosses borders more readily these days than ever before.

FURTHER INFORMATION

The magazines *Spain* and *Living in Spain* are published and sold in the UK. They are a valuable source of information. Money transfer organisations, banks, building societies and financial advisors advertise regularly. So do contributors on legal matters.

Financial advice in the UK: www.fsa.gov.uk

Financial advice in Spain: www.cnmv.es

5
Professional People

INTRODUCTION

What is the difference between an *abogado* and a notary? Who is a *gestor* and what does an *asesor fiscal* do? Does a *notario* only rubber stamp documents? Most foreigners, especially those taking up residence, will meet at least one of these highly regarded professionals, so it is important to know what they do.

ABOGADO

There are many people engaged in the highly respected profession of a solicitor/lawyer who in Spain is called an *abogado*. They are admired for their ability to deal with Spanish law, where complex legal, procedural and administrative issues can bog down everyday affairs. It is best to deal with an *abogado* who speaks English well. In legal situations a working knowledge of Spanish is not good enough.

What do they do?

- Upon buying a property they will handle everything from drawing up the initial contract through to accompanying the purchaser and seller to the notary's office.

They will check that nothing is wrong by making sure that there are no outstanding debts on the property and that non-standard clauses, designed to catch the unwary, do not appear in the contract.

- Where an off plan purchase is involved they will again check the contract and ensure that stage payments, which are common in this case, are correct.

- They will act with a *poder* (power of attorney) to buy and sell.

- They draw up wills and distribute the estate on death.

- They do everything that a UK solicitor could do from divorce through to criminal proceedings.

Generally, the fees charged are less than those of the equivalent in the UK. The *Colegio de Abogadaos* publishes a list of minimum fees that can be charged. The legal profession is a competitive business and most of the time a client is charged a minimum fee.

The relationship between an *abogado* and a notary (see later) needs some explanation. A notary will register a document provided it meets all the necessary legal criteria. They may even give some advice to the *abogado* on, for example, drawing up wills. But it is the *abogado* who, in the first instance, considers for the client all the legal options, draws up the documents to be registered and explains the legal ins and outs.

ASESOR FISCAL

This is an accountant for people running a business and for anyone resident or non-resident who declares any income tax to the *Hacienda*. They are used by anyone not wanting to complete these tasks personally for there is no legal requirement to employ an *asesor fiscal*. Only a foreigner afflicted by the noon day sun would attempt to fill out tax forms and, since taxes have to be assessed for everyone, almost everyone has an *asesor fiscal*. A good one will always keep the client informed of tax regulations and legitimate ways of reducing any tax liability.

GESTOR

A *gestor* acts as an intermediary between Spanish officialdom and the general public, being a registered agent dealing with government departments. It says much about the Spanish way of life that such a person is necessary to deal with its bureaucracy.

They are competent, highly qualified administrators but what do they do? For the Spanish they simply deal with the complicated mass of paperwork. For foreigners they do the same, in a country where the language barrier, a new culture and complicated procedures cause additional problems. Some of the tasks covered by a *gestor* are:

- application for *NIE* and residency;

- gaining entry into the Spanish health system;

- dealing with the payment of car tax, car transfer tax and other car related matters;

- help in setting up new businesses.

A *gestor* does no more than a member of the public can do themselves, but they do it for a number of people who have paid to have it done efficiently. Some people say, rather sheepishly, that a *gestor* is employed by people who have more money than time! But they know the ins and outs of the system and get the job done. State bureaucrats like a *gestor* too, as they know all the forms will be completed correctly.

NOTARIO

A notary is a qualified *abogado* who has studied to become a notary. The public notary is an official who cannot be employed nor instructed to act for an individual. The *notario* represents the State. They do not guarantee or verify statements or check contractual terms. They protect the interests of the individual by pointing out any pitfalls, by offering advice on legal points and volunteering information. Although some are bilingual, they are not expected to speak any language other than their native tongue or to explain the complexities of Spanish law.

A notary's main task is to make sure that documents are legalised. This includes power of attorney, wills, certifying copies of passports, registering company charters, stamping the official minutes of a Community of Property Owners, notarising a letter and, most commonly, approving the deed of a property known as the *escritura*.

Most people meet the notary for the first time when concluding the purchase of a property. The *escritura* is signed and witnessed by the *notario* in the presence of the seller(s) and the purchaser(s) unless any party has utilised a power of attorney to excuse their own presence. The *notario*'s duty is to:

- Check the name of the title holder and whether there are any charges or encumbrances against the property.

- Check the contents of the *escritura* and ensure it is read to the purchaser(s) prior to signing.

- Check that both parties have been advised of their legal obligations.

- Certify the *escritura* has been signed and the money paid.

- Warn parties if they knowingly undervalue the purchase price of a property by more than 20 per cent, and ensure five per cent of the purchase price is withheld and paid to the *Hacienda* if a property is sold by a non-resident.

OVERLAPPING ROLES

The role of an *abogado*, *asesor fiscal* and *gestor* can overlap. For example all can obtain an *NIE* and *residencia*. In fact the first one visited will need an *NIE*. Whose door is knocked on first? Usually an *abogado*, as they are part of the property buying process. Like any good businessperson, the *abogado* will seek to retain a future relationship with their clients after property conveyancing has been completed. There are taxes to be dealt with, wills to be prepared, possibly a driving licence and transfer and entry into the medical system.

It certainly is convenient to have a one-stop-shop for all administrative, legal and fiscal affairs. Cost comes into it too and most people find it better to use an *abogado* or an *asesor fiscal* or a *gestor* separately, as appropriate to the task.

FURTHER INFORMATION

The *abogado*, *asesor fiscal*, *gestor* and *notario* all belong to their respective organisations called a *colegio*. They can be readily accessed on the web, in Spanish of course, by words such as *colegio de abogados de valencia*.

6
Purchasing a Property

INTRODUCTION

It is an established fact – in the last 20 years Spanish house prices have risen faster than anywhere else in the world. They have risen by about 18 per cent per year and experts predict this trend will continue for the immediate future.

Irrespective of inflation, it is important to realise that property buying procedures are different in Spain. Forget the traditional approach of putting in an offer, arranging a mortgage and asking a solicitor to sort things out. Prospective buyers must carry out research and ask questions themselves, rather than assuming a solicitor will deal with all these matters. You need to learn about the contract, the *escritura* and other legal documents. It is also necessary to understand the Spanish conveyancing system from start to finish, as it can trap the unwary in a country where there are many property horror stories.

BACK TO BASICS

When it's for sale a property located in Spain will be in one of two classifications:

- moveable property (*bienes muebles*)

- and immovable property (*bienes inmuebles*).

This is a similar definition to the concept of personal effects and immovable property. Immovable property includes land and buildings, but not the shares in a company owning land and buildings.

Land ownership is freehold. It is possible to own a building or even part of a building separately from land itself, as in the case of apartments which are owned freehold.

Where a building or piece of land is physically divided between a number of people a *comunidad de propietarios* is formed. The *comunidad* is divided into privately owned parts such as an individual flat, and communally owned areas such as gardens and swimming pool.

Rights, but not ownership, can exist over land such as *caminos*, paths, rights of way, tenancies and life interests. They require some formal agreement to ensure their validity.

FINDING A PROPERTY

Estate agents

By virtue of their daily contacts, estate agents know who are buying and selling. The top agents keep files of buyers, sellers and properties. It is not unusual for a good agent, when they learn of a new listing, to sell it within 24 hours to a buyer they know will buy that type of property. An agent, given time and a detailed specification, will always find a property for a determined buyer. They may have to be chased occasionally, but that is part of the process of being determined.

Spanish estate agents have a curious name – *inmobiliaria*, a word almost suggesting that 'a person does not move'. Yet in Spain these people are very common – small local estate agents who know their patch well, concentrating mainly on resale properties. They need not be Spanish and indeed many on the Costas are German, Scandinavian or British.

It is a good idea to deal with a registered estate agent. In Spain they belong to the

Agente de Propiedad Inmobiliaria, have a certificate of registration and an identification number. They can be sued if anything goes wrong. Dealing with such a registered business gives the purchaser more security and confidence.

There have always been stories in Spain of people losing their life savings because they have dealt with an unscrupulous estate agent. The only real way to avoid this is to deal with a registered agent whose number should be on a sign outside the office, or on a window display, or on the exterior of the building.

The quality of estate agents has vastly improved in the last few years. Selling houses attracts some of the finest people. But it still attracts some of the more unscrupulous characters too, probably because it is possible to earn a handsome income without working too hard. Due to its financial structure the estate agency business opens doors to all types of people some of whom are not completely honest. However most agents aren't thieves and swindlers, if anything they're more honest than the average person because they have their business reputations to protect.

UK agents

Estate agents based outside Spain offer three-day, escorted and highly focused inspection visits. The flights are cheap, there is a hotel booked and entertainment is laid on. Viewing is from the comfort of a mini-bus with only a short stroll to each show house. The ambience of the area is highlighted. From the properties shown most people can decide what is best for their own circumstances. It is however a highly pressurised trip, where time and space to think are at a premium. It does not give freedom to appreciate the bigger picture, or the true ambience of the town or countryside. It is a snapshot at a point in time and far from being an inspection trip it is a highly pressurised sales trip.

Before travelling people are reminded of the currency and deposit arrangements required to reserve a property. This is sales pressure at its highest, for potential purchasers are signing a reservation contract (see later in this chapter) and paying a deposit without the benefit of the contract being checked by an *abogado*. It can be said, however, that these international agents are quite reliable.

Public auctions

A bank foreclosing on a property can result in a court ordered property auction. On occasions an auction can also be voluntary. Low prices can make auctions attractive. Prices are low because in judicial auctions the process is intended to recover debts and once these and costs have been recovered there is little reason for auctioneers to press for a higher price. Interested in buying a property at an auction? Auctions ordered by a court (*subasta*) and non-judicial auctions are advertised in the press. While brief details of properties are published, to make any decision a pre-auction inspection is essential.

Get someone to assist on the day of the auction too, someone who will explain precisely what needs to be done at each stage. Set a maximum price to be offered. A refundable deposit is levied by the auctioneer allowing the entry of a bid. Have a ten per cent deposit (less the bidding deposit) to hand when a bid is accepted.

SETTING PRIORITIES

All legal procedures and documents are important. All property purchasing documents are important. Failure to understand one may have serious consequences. Property documents can be broken down into four groupings.

1   Pre-purchase checks.

2   Signing a reservation contract or contract.

3   Pre-*escritura* for new properties.

4   *Escritura* and beyond.

All pre-purchase checks need to be completed before signing anything. Signing a contract signifies this has been done and everything is in order. An *escritura* merely legalises what has gone before. A contract, signed soon after the start of the buying process, is therefore the most important document in the property buying process. A good contract, correctly worded, is of benefit to both the buyer and seller. Altering a contract is almost impossible. A bad contract creates unnecessary difficulties. Reneging on a contract means losing a deposit.

PRE-PURCHASE CHECKS

An architect's drawing

It makes sense to have a plan of a house, particularly for a relatively new property or one bought off plan (not yet built). What is required is neither a glossy brochure, nor a three-dimensional sketch or artist's impression, but an architect's plan showing the dimensions of each floor and each room in square metres. With new properties this is a legal requirement with the living space in each room, the total build area and plot size all specified. The overall size of the property, again measured in square metres, determines its market price, its valuation for any mortgage, insurance premiums and an assessment for local taxes.

Plan parcial

It also makes sense, when buying land or a new property yet to be built, to have a line drawing locating the plot. This is called *plan parcial*, a Spanish term meaning a plan of parcels or plots of land, which is registered with the planning department at the local town hall. It ensures land or property for sale is approved and registered with the town hall and also shows other adjacent developments or roads planned close by. While a line drawing supplied by the builder's architect will suffice on most occasions, a *plan parcial* from the *Urbanismo Department* at the *Ayuntamiento* (town hall) is the only approved legal source. Prospective purchasers should also be aware of developments close to the sea which need to be approved by the *Jefatura de Costas* as well as the town hall. Spain's 1988 *Ley de Costas*, or Law of Coasts, empowers the authorities to restrict building and to control height and density within 100 metres of the high-water mark.

Nota Simple

This very important document is often overlooked. Translated it means a 'simple note' which is issued by the Land Registry Office and is a copy of the Property Registration details (see *Registro de la Propiedad* later in this chapter). For a property yet to be constructed, it is proof that the person selling is the registered owner of the land and that there are no debts on the land. For an existing property it shows details of the present owner, if the property has an outstanding mortgage or loan, or if it has any debts registered against it.

Obtaining a copy of the *Nota Simple* is straightforward. Firstly locate the Registry Office with jurisdiction over the property or land. This is not always in the nearest town or village. Secondly complete a request for information form and pay a small fee, then return in a few days to collect the *Nota Simple*.

Establishing the right to sell

While the *Nota Simple* will give ownership details of an existing title, it makes sense that further documents are requested to establish the person selling has the right to do so. Details in the *escritura*, passport or *residencia* number and *Certificado de Empadronamiento* should all agree with the facts in the *Nota Simple*. If not there is something wrong. An examination of property dimensions recorded in the *escritura* should also be the same as the actual property – if not an illegal alteration has taken place.

Quota of community charges

Buying a property in Spain, particularly on an urbanisation or in an apartment block, invariably means becoming a member of a community of property owners. A country property or a town house in a street will not have to deal with community issues.

It is advisable to at least understand approximate community costs involved prior to signing a contract, but in most situations this would not materialistically affect a buying decision. Indeed, with a very new project an overall community budget will not have been determined. Conversely with an established community the costs, constitution, chairman and committee members will all be established.

The allocation of costs will vary. On an urbanisation of 1,000 homes of equal size, each will carry a charge of 0.1 per cent of total expenditure. If however the urbanisation had 500 large and 500 small homes the allocation could be 0.125 per cent and 0.075 per cent respectively. This allocation of costs, called a quota and expressed as a percentage of total community costs, is determined at a very early stage in any new development. The information should be available upon signing a contract.

Debts

Spain's laws carry any debt on a property over to the new owner. Prior to signing the contract a check has to be made to ensure there are no encumbrances such as mortgages, or outstanding debts such as local taxes and community charges, and all service bills have been paid in full. A mortgage or loan is repaid at the notary. The following is a process for checking this:

- A copy of the *Nota Simple* will tell if there are any mortgages or loans against the property. A seller is not trusted to pay off a mortgage of their own accord, so it must be paid at the time of signing the *escritura*.

- Enquire at the town hall to check any unpaid local taxes, *Impuesto Sobre Bienes Inmuebles* (*IBI*).

- Enquire through the Community of Owners, or their management company, to ascertain all community charges have been paid.

- Check receipts provided by the seller that all bills for electricity, water and telephone have been paid.

A first time buyer probably does not have time or local knowledge to carry out these checks. An agent should do this, but often does not. A notary will carry out some of these checks. An *abogado* will do a fine job as their professional reputation is at risk. But a bank manager issuing a mortgage will do it even better since the bank's money is at risk. *Remember, all unpaid debts on a property are inherited by the buyer.*

Impuesto Sobre Bienes Inmuebles (IBI) and *valor catastral*

An *IBI* receipt is not available for a new property, but is available from the town hall for a resale property. The *IBI* receipt will show the property's *catastral* reference number and the *valor catastral*, the official assessed value used in calculating *IBI*. The assessed value is usually substantially less than the real market value.

The *Catastro* is a second system of property registration, defining the location, physical description and boundaries of a property which unlike the Property Registry concentrates on ownership and title. Both systems should of course agree. What is in the *escritura* should be in the *Castrol Certificate*. Sometimes the boundaries of a property, or even the property itself, can differ because people have accepted descriptions made in one document but not in the other.

Although the Certificate comes in two parts, one is a description in words and the other a plan or photo; this can be bypassed by a clerk at the efficient SUMA offices (where they exist) demonstrating relevant details on a computer, avoiding the inevitable form filling, cost and delay.

SIGNING THE CONTRACT

Reservation Contract

This document, sometimes referred to as a Pre-Contract, represents the first step in the buying process for a new property – a property bought off plan. It will usually necessitate the payment of a non-returnable reservation fee, which is included in the initial deposit. It is an outline agreement to reserve the property and should contain as minimum the following details.

- Name, address and passport number of the purchaser.

- Name, address and the business or personal identification of the agent or developer or both.

- House type, plot number and address of the property.

- The price in euros. This should clearly state if *IVA* (Value Added Tax) is included in the price.

- The reservation deposit and payment formulae.

- Signature of both parties and date.

Purchase Contract

To repeat – a Purchase Contract is the most important document in the Spanish property buying process. It will repeat information in a Pre-Contract, adding greater detail. Signing a Contract signifies the following:

- The plan of the house and location of the plot are satisfactory.

- The *Nota Simple* has been checked, is in order and the person selling has the right to do so.

- The Contract has been read and understood.

- Signing the Contract triggers the release of a normally non-returnable cash deposit.

- The purchaser has the necessary monies, or mortgage, available to complete the transaction.

A contract should be well written and comprehensive. It is normally in Spanish but on some occasions can be set out paragraph by paragraph in Spanish and the mother tongue of the purchaser, ensuring no ambiguity. The key points are:

- It reconfirms all previous details, namely the parties to the agreement; the ownership of the land, its registration and freedom from debts; details of the plot; the size and description of the property. The seller is the owner of the property, not an estate agent handling the deal.

- It sets out in detail the method, dates, currency, price and payment schedule; financial penalties for failing to complete and any charges for connecting water and electricity.

- Where appropriate, it confirms that a purchaser respects the obligations of law surrounding the Community of Owners and gives details of a nominated district court should things go wrong.

- It sets out any special clauses such as 'Subject to obtaining a mortgage'.

Two types of Purchase Contract

A Full Preliminary Contract (*Contrato Privado de Compraventa*) is the most common type of document. It is called a private contract because it is freely agreed between the buyer and seller in the presence of an *abogado*. It is an agreement to commit both parties. The seller must sell and the buyer must buy subject to the conditions they agree.

An Option Contract should be avoided. This is a written document in which the seller agrees to take a stated property off the market for a fixed period and to sell it at a stated price to a stated person at anytime within a stated period. It lacks definition, is a standard form completed by an agent and not checked by an *abogado*.

PRE-*ESCRITURA* – FOR NEW PROPERTIES

Certificado Final de la Direccion de la Obra

Translated this simply means Certificate of the Termination of the Building. It does not mean the building is falling down, quite the opposite in fact. It is a Certificate produced by the architect when a new house is finally complete. It enables a declaration of a new building to be made at the notary's office and is used to obtain the *Licencia de Primera Ocupacion* detailed below.

Licencia de Primera Ocupacion

The Licence of First Occupation is obtained from the town hall on production of the *Cerificado Final de la Direccion de la Obra*. It is a licence to inhabit the property, and registers it for the purpose of local taxes and the connection of services. The electrical supply company will not connect to an unregistered property.

On new developments the initial supply of water from external pipes and electricity without meters is often obtained from a builder's supply point. The reason for this is simple. The completion and occupation of property is faster than the ability of utility companies to connect their supplies.

Building insurance

A new property will be insured by a builder during construction and at a low nominal value for 12 months from the date of occupation. A copy of this policy should be available, stating the insured value and what exactly it covers. When a house is occupied, a top up building policy is all that is required for the first year. It is obviously sound practice to have an additional household insurance protecting against damage or theft and against claims by others. This is important if absent from a property for a long period – such as with holiday homes.

ESCRITURA AND BEYOND

Power of attorney

This simple mechanism is useful if a purchaser cannot be in Spain when the legal paperwork requires completion. If the property is in joint names and one person cannot attend, then a power of attorney is essential. People on holiday can avoid weary queues at the *notario* by delegating the power of attorney to a legal representative.

- A **special power of attorney** can only deal with the buying or selling of property.

- A **general power of attorney** can deal with almost anything but is likely to embrace loans, mortgages and bank accounts.

To draw up a power of attorney, visit the local notary's office with your passport, and details of who the power of attorney is 'for' and who it is given 'to', together with a payment of approximately 50 euros. A few days later the document will be ready for signature.

If a power of attorney is required it does make sense to have it drawn up at the onset of a purchase, but of course it is possible to conclude such an authorisation at any time. The Spanish Consulate will assist too in giving details of solicitors who are authorised to prepare a power of attorney in any country. Signing the document in a Spanish Consulate in the UK is regarded as if it had been signed in Spain.

Escritura

The end product of a visit to the *notario* is the *escritura*. It is a hard backed copy, covered in official stamps, signatures and writing. It is typed on thick, numbered paper. It is an impressive document produced to a standard format. All *escrituras* start with the date, the name of the notary and the *Protocal* number which is effectively the filing reference should another copy be required. The *escritura* is the deed for a property. It is a record of the property at a point in time.

There are three versions of the *escritura*.

- The *Copia Simple* (not to be confused with *Nota Simple*) is a copy of the *escritura*, less the signatures, which is sufficient to prove ownership. It is available on the day of signing at the notary and is recognised as suitable for most legal purposes. It is normal for the purchaser to hold a copy of this document.

- The *Escritura de Compraventa* is the main document signed in the notary's office.

- The *Escritura Publica* is the *Escritura de Compraventa* complete with its many official stamps from the Property Resister, which converts it into a public document.

An authorised *abogado*, or the property owner, or in the case of a mortgage a bank, can hold the *escritura*, but irrespective of who holds it someone has to collect the finished document from the notary. Thousands of *escrituras* lie gathering dust in notaries' offices, uncollected or unregistered because of some minor technicality. In the latter case the property will remain unregistered until the 'problem' has been rectified.

The document itself is written in legalised Spanish making literal translation almost impossible. The owner never holds the original deed, but only the first authorised copy. The original is always held at the notary's office. A second authorised copy can be requested in the event of the first being lost.

No one can doubt the necessity of having a comprehensive document, particularly one which clearly states debts or mortgages, or indeed the transparency of having this document made public. But there is considerable ceremony associated with its preparation and signing which many people believe to be unnecessary. It certainly legalises a situation but it does not alter or undo anything that may have been agreed previously at the contract stage.

Registro de la Propiedad

This is the last piece of paper in the buying cycle. Strangely it is not the *Escritura Publica* that is the final step, as it is registered with the Property Register being over-stamped *Registro de la Propiedad*. This simple, one-page document simply closes the loop to the *Nota Simple* which was considered at the start of the buying cycle. What does all this mean? The *Registro de la Propiedad* registers the property in a public place, giving details of who has the title, which notary was responsible for the *escritura* and listing details of mortgages or loans.

Licencia de Obras

Let us assume that a property built to a correct specification requires a small modification such as a dividing wall between an adjacent property and perhaps a shed to hold some tools.

Do you need permission to do this? The answer is yes. In fact permission is usually quite straightforward. A visit to the town hall, the completion of a paper entitled *Solicitud de Licencia de Obras*, clearly marked minor, and the payment of a small fee, will result in the necessary approval. That is of course provided the modification fits in with the overall urbanisation design, style and specification.

Further information on licences and builders are contained in Chapter 8.

BUYING WITHOUT AN *ESCRITURA*

There are situations where a property can be purchased without an *escritura* for perfectly legitimate reasons. However, this is not a permanent situation.

Fast-track conveyancing is one such situation. In some areas of Spain, especially around the southern end of the Costa Blanca, the whole infrastructure is devoted to marketing new property yet to be constructed – buying off plan. Here procedures involving the purchase of new properties have been speeded up. Fast-track conveyancing is different from the standard procedure as time is important and no one wishes to be held up waiting for legal matters to be completed. So the final payment is made direct to the builder, possession taken immediately and the parties to the purchase sort out the paperwork (*escritura*) at a later date.

A second common situation arises when a *nota simple* states the property is owned by 'Heirs of Senor …' Or the owners of rural land are brothers and sisters whose family has owned the land for years without a written document. A solution for property with no registered title is to obtain from the Property Registry a 'negative certificate' which means the Registry has no recorded owner of the property. The buyer requests the property be registered in their name and the seller justifies their title by any documentary evidence possible. The proceedings are published in case anyone wishes to protest. If not, in one year the *escritura* is finalised.

A more complex process, involving investigation and court action, is called the *Expediente de Dominio*, which is used to establish a title when a property is registered, but in the name of a person who no longer claims it, perhaps because the original owner has died. The claim is published and evidence taken to a court for it to rule on ownership.

Yet another reason for buying without an *escritura* is holding an off plan property on a private contract. In this case a purchaser buys a partly built property on a private contract from a developer and sells it on at a profit before completion, thus avoiding taxes. In a fast moving property market, where properties are bought for investment, they can change hands quickly and are not registered. Investors wait for the next buyer to come along and complete in the normal way. Owning a property on a private contract without an *escritura* means a property cannot be seized by a court in order to pay a debt, it avoids taxes and conceals an asset from any interested parties.

GET ADVICE

While conveyancing procedures in some countries have one solicitor representing the buyer and another solicitor representing the seller, it is not necessary in Spain to have two *abogados*. It is accepted that only one is necessary, as a contract drawn up by an *abogado* can be assumed to be correct. After all, the final legal safeguard, a notary, is still to come. But here in lies a contradiction!

An agent selling a property normally appoints the *abogado*. The agent knows the area, who is available and who they have worked with before. The contract may be perfectly legal but it is possible it will contain clauses more favourable to the seller than the buyer. If an *abogado* is dealing with hundreds of contracts on behalf of a builder or agent, where will their loyalties lie?

Conversely a person buying a property may be new to the district, probably does not know an *abogado* and can easily go along with this arrangement. But who pays the bill? The buyer. So it is wise for a buyer rather than the agent to appoint the *abogado* who draws up the contract. If that is not practicable then a buyer should take additional independent legal advice from another *abogado* prior to signing the contract. So we are back to having two lawyers!

The importance of legal advice

It cannot be emphasised too strongly that anyone planning to buy a property in Spain should take legal advice in a language in which they are fluent, from a lawyer experienced in Spanish property law. Always deal with professionals and do not assume that by dealing with a fellow countryman the advice is better, cheaper or even unbiased. Consult an *abogado* to check draft documents. Does the person have the right to sell? Have all the permissions been granted? Are there any debts? Is the Contract in order or does it contain non-standard clauses? What are the payment schedules? Do penalty clauses exist for a builder failing to complete a new property on time?

Problems associated with purchasing a property abroad have been highlighted many times in the popular press. From a legal viewpoint Spain has not always been the safest place to buy. Most horror stories come at the start of the buying process. It is at the contract and deposit stage that things go wrong, where insufficient checks have been made, or inadequate procedures followed. Among the myriad of problems experienced by buyers in Spain the most prominent are:

- unscrupulous agents;

- people absconding with the deposit;

- properties bought without legal title;

- issues surrounding developers and builders, such as lack of planning permission or bankruptcy;

- undischarged loans or mortgage from the previous owner;

- off plan properties not being completed on time;

- an altered property bearing no resemblance to that described in the *escritura*.

Do not sign anything, or pay a deposit, until legal advice has been sought. Once the advice is given – take it. Do not assume it is someone dotting the I's and crossing the T's. One of the most common phrases heard in Spain is about buyers 'leaving their brains behind at the airport'. It is true! The rush to buy a dream home, or a pressurised selling trip, or even the euphoria of a moment often make people do incredibly stupid things, literally handing over cash deposits to agents or owners with little or no security.

FURTHER READING

Harry King, *Buying a Property in Spain*. Oxford: How to Books, endorsed by the *Daily Telegraph*.

Rider, Holtom and Howell, *Buying a Property in Spain*. London: Cadogan Guides, endorsed by the *Sunday Times*.

David Hampshire, *Buying a Home in Spain*. London: Survival Guides.

7
Paying for a Property

INTRODUCTION

This chapter deals with payment procedures and costs involved in purchasing a property. Perhaps of greater interest, it exposes an unofficial practice called black money and how to respond to it. One almost forgotten decision involves different options for who actually owns a property. With a combination of Spanish and UK inheritance tax systems, getting ownership wrong can be a very expensive mistake.

PAYING THE MONEY

Stage payments for a new property purchased off plan

Example 1: British developer	Example 2: German developer	Example 3: Spanish developer
10% reservation contract	40% on signing contract	3% reservation contract
40% stage payment	60% on completion	16% on signing contract
25% stage payment		14 *letras* each of 1.5%
25% on completion		60% on completion

In all three examples *IVA* is included in the price and paid at the various stages. The Spanish developer uses the peculiarly Spanish system of *letras* (see Chapter 4).

Payments for a resale property

5% to 10% on signing a contract

90% to 95% on completion

IVA – paid on completion.

A partly built property

50% on signing a contract (walls, roof, windows and doors completed)

20% stage payment

20% on completion

10% retained for up to one year to cover snagging defects

IVA – paid on completion.

The basic rules

- All payments can be negotiated. Remember a contract is a private agreement between a buyer and a seller and cannot be overruled.

- If the buyer fails to complete, deposits are non-returnable unless there is a clause in the contract to the contrary. If a seller fails to complete the transaction the buyer is recompensed to a value twice the amount of the deposit unless the contract states otherwise.

- If a builder fails to deliver a new property on time penalty charges accrue. These should be stated in the contract.

- Property sales between individuals follow a system of private contract and deposit(s), followed by the notary and final payment. There is nothing binding about this. If everyone agrees it is perfectly possible to go direct to the notary, pay the money and obtain the *escritura*.

ALLOWING FOR ADDITIONAL BUYING COSTS

It is normal to allow ten per cent of the property value declared in the *escritura* for the additional buying costs which covers three taxes, two fees and charges from an *abogado*.

- Transfer Tax or *IVA* (Value Added Tax)   7%

- *Actos Juridicos Documentados* on a new property only   1.0%

- *Plus Valia* Tax   0.5%

- Notary fees   0.5%

- Property Registry fees   0.5%

- Charges from an *abogado*   1.0%

Transfer Tax and *IVA*

Impuesto de Transmisiones Patrimoniales is the Spanish for Transfer Tax which is charged on a sale between two individuals. *IVA*, the Spanish equivalent of Value Added Tax, is a business charge on a sale between, say, a property company and an individual. Governments can vary taxes, and they do, but it is normal to allow seven per cent for either of these two taxes.

Actos Juridicos Documentados

Effectively stamp duty of one per cent payable on a new property. It is not payable on a resale property.

Plus Valia tax

Plus Valia is payable on a resale property and a new property. It is assessed locally on an increase in the value of the land since the previous owner bought the property or a developer bought the land. An apartment on an urbanisation where little land is involved, or where there has been no increase in value in a short time, will occur a low *plus valia* tax charge. Conversely a home with a large plot of land, held by the previous owner for say 30 years, will suffer a high charge.

Of course it is the seller who should pay this tax. They have gained the benefit of the increase in land value. The law of the country supports this view. In practice however this tax has often fallen on the purchaser since it a more secure method of collection. After all, a vendor may flee the country leaving this tax unpaid.

A purchaser may feel, quite rightly, aggrieved at paying this tax. A recourse is simply to have a clause inserted in the contract stating it is the vendor who pays the *Plus Valia* tax and withholding this sum from the final payment.

Notary fees

These vary according to the value of the property declared in the *escritura* and the number of pages in the document. Allow 350 euros or 0.5 per cent.

Property registry

Again there is a fee to have the property registered. It is wise to allow a similar figure of 0.5 per cent.

Charges from the *abogado*

Naturally this fee will depend on the amount of work done. If the basic paperwork has been handled to a straightforward conclusion then the charge will be low. If on the other hand there has been complications or the need to draw up multilingual contracts then the charges will be higher. Allow one per cent for this charge.

Who pays?

The buyer and seller can agree between themselves who pays taxes, fees and charges. This can be incorporated into the contract and is not overridden by Spanish law. In practice however the buyer pays either directly, or on occasions indirectly, when the agent incorporates these charges into an overall selling price. *Todos los gastos* is the Spanish phrase meaning 'all expenses arising'.

It is also normal practice to deposit the approximate figure of ten per cent of the *escritura* value with the *abogado* or the bank manager (for mortgaged properties), who will pay these accounts on behalf of the buyer who submits an itemised statement when the transactions are completed.

BLACK MONEY

It is quite common in Spain to have two purchase prices for a property:

- one price is the actual price paid exclusive of any fees or taxes;

- the other is a lower price declared in the *escritura*;

- as a guideline, the difference between the two prices should be less than 15 to 20 per cent;

- the difference between the two prices is normally paid to the vendor in cash.

This practice is known to agents, buyers and sellers, builders and developers, the *abogado,* the bank manager and the notary. It is known by the tax authorities. In fact it is known by everyone.

It is a mechanism of tax evasion which if not radically abused, is tolerated by the Spanish tax man. All taxes and fees are calculated on the value stated in the *escritura*, not the actual price paid. The Transfer Tax or *IVA* charged at seven per cent is effectually reduced to 5.6 per cent if the *escritura* value is declared at 80 per cent of true selling value. When reselling the same property a few years later a similar reduction needs to be applied to avoid excessive payment of capital gains tax as this too is based on a value declared in the *escritura*.

Many people are now seeing the folly of this practice but once started it is difficult to stop. The saving of say 1.4 per cent in initial taxes on purchasing can easily be outweighed by a greater loss in capital gains on any profit made when reselling. If a low value is declared on purchase then the capital gains liability will be on a greater profit upon selling. It is in the interests of the buyer to declare the full value of the sale.

Spanish tax officers do not sit idly by. Renowned for being sharp but pragmatic, they maintain their own table of property values and are empowered to set a higher value which can result in an additional tax bill should they feel excessive tax avoidance has taken place. This scrutiny is applied mainly, but not exclusively, to a purchaser's tax liability. If they discover that the sale has been under declared by more than 20 per cent they can apply heavy penalties under the terms of Spain's *Ley de Tasas* which was enacted to prevent this practice.

'Black' is the term used to describe the difference between the actual price paid and the value declared in the *escritura*. 'Black money' describes a cash payment representing the difference in values. Incidentally the payment of 'black money' can also occur at the start of the buying process, when an initial deposit paid as cash to the agent becomes their black money commission.

MINIMISING THE RISK OF LOSING MONEY

- Never pay a deposit directly to a seller. They may abscond. Never pay a deposit to an agent. They too may abscond. The agent will want the deposit paid to them in cash. But it is not their house! It is not their money. Ensure a deposit is placed in a bonded client account, from which it will not be released until the sale is final.

- Pay by cheque or a certified cheque or a banker's draft in euros drawn from a Spanish bank account. Do not pay in cash.

- Never make a cheque out to an agent, only to a seller (reservation contract excepted).

- If the seller insists on anonymity ensure that no money changes hands until at the notary – where a seller must be identified.

- Be fully aware if the deposit is returnable or non-returnable in the event of failing to complete a transaction. Alternatively ask the number of day's grace in which to change your mind.

- Do not accept a verbal agreement – ask to see it in writing.

- The payment of a deposit is the first financial and legal step in buying a property. It must be linked to a contract.

WHO SHOULD OWN IT?

There is more than one option when structuring ownership of a property. Each has advantages and disadvantages. The choice depends on personal circumstances, together with due consideration of inheritance tax. It is an important choice, for if incorrect more tax will be paid than necessary both during a lifetime and on death. Inheritance tax consequences arise not only in Spain but back home too.

Joint ownership

This is the normal way of proceeding. Two people buying together will buy in both names. It gives a level of security. Upon death the other half passes to the fellow owner (UK inheritance law) and is taxed according to the relationship by Spanish inheritance laws. It is normal for the ownership split to be 50/50 but in the case of a second marriage with three children on one side and one child on the other the split can be 75/25 which would give a fairer distribution of inheritance.

Children named in the deed

In the example above, with two adults and four children, there is nothing wrong with having all six names on the deed in equal or unequal parts. It one person dies their share of the property passes equally to the other five. Spanish inheritance tax will be small if anything.

And the disadvantage – if the children fall out with the surviving spouse they could insist on a sale of the property unless an arrangement was made for the spouse retaining a life interest.

Property in children's name

In this case a property is in the name of the children only, with a life interest held by the named parents who paid for it in the first place. The property is the children's in whatever parts so defined. A life interest (*usufructo*) is the right to use the property for a lifetime. On the death of one person, the remaining spouse or partner who has a life interest would still be able to use it. On death there will be little or no inheritance tax.

A disadvantage – the property is no longer owned by the purchaser and if families fall out, get divorced or children suddenly die it becomes complicated. As this is a peculiarly Spanish practice there is plenty of 'civil code' for guidance.

Offshore company

A property may be owned by an offshore registered company, in a so called tax haven, where the property is not in the name of the owner but in the name of a company. The owner of the company owns the property. When the property is sold, it is only company shares that are transferred. The same company continues to own the same Spanish property, so no Spanish taxes are charged. But the company has a new owner.

A similar approach applies to inheritance tax – the company is bequeathed to an inheritor. The Spanish authorities, blocking this loophole, have placed a tax of three per cent per annum on any property held by an offshore company. After three years it is cheaper to pay the taxes associated with purchase (ten per cent) and after ten years probably better to allow for inheritance tax at 30 per cent.

8
Doing it Yourself

INTRODUCTION

Foreigners purchasing a property in Spain predominantly buy a new home bought off plan, or a resale home. There are however three other combinations:

- picking a plot of land and model property design from an agent, developer or builder;

- renovating a ruin – the classic rural *finca*;

- going it alone, building it yourself, on rural land.

Building or redeveloping a home is not something to be taken on lightly. It is not a case of buying land, approving a design, appointing a builder, going away and maintaining telephone contact. You need to be personally involved or, failing that, to ensure the project is managed by a local architect or building engineer. Before starting on a project of this scale appoint a good *abogado*, one who can recommend a builder and an architect and who can also assist with a building permit and planning application.

PLOT OF LAND WITH A MODEL PROPERTY

There is little difference between this approach and buying a standard property off plan. A plot of land will be a choice from a plan. The house type will be a choice of several options available from a builder – type A, or type B, etc. With some thought and attention to detail a dream house is possible but personal supervision of the building programme is absolutely necessary – location of the plot, position of the property on the plot and adherence to the building specification.

RENOVATED OR RESTORED HOUSES

Many people like the idea of returning a derelict ruin to its former glory. Restoration is less popular than building new, because it is usually more expensive and there are limited opportunities to acquire a cheap, suitable shell building. Do not purchase a picturesque tumbledown farmhouse only to discover that renovation is way beyond personal skills and means. You could also get hopelessly bogged down in trying to get planning permission and satisfying all the requirements of building regulations. It is all too easy to become entangled in red tape if not conversant with Spanish laws, nor speaking the language fluently.

Whatever the disrepair of a building, the process starts with the purchase of a property. It may be run down. It may even be a ruin. It is probably in the country but can be a terraced house in a Spanish town. Either way, the starting point is the purchase of a resale property.

Carrying out checks

Since the external structure of the building will probably be altered a number of checks need to be carried out before purchasing. The most obvious is to check with the planning department at the town hall to find out exactly what can be done. Demolish, rebuild, extend upwards or outwards, or simply renovate, are the options. With a town house, renovation and an upward extension are probably the only possibilities.

In the country do not assume anything is possible. In fact the height, size and number of properties per 1,000 or 10,000 or 30,000 square metres is regulated by a town hall planning department and it may only be possible to extend the footprint of a property by a small amount. Ten thousand square metres of land is a normal requirement for *rustico* properties (country land with no building designation with a water supply) and 30,000 square metres for land without a water supply.

Check utility supplies. If none, how much will it cost to install them? Important questions need answering about supply of electricity and water, sewage disposal, TV reception, telephone and communication systems.

In the UK it is normal to have a building survey on a property prior to exchange of contracts. Some UK surveyors operate in Spain, providing a survey to cover all structural elements, such as the roof, walls, doors, windows, floors, outbuildings, garden walls and external and internal decorative state. Damp tests will be carried out by an electronic damp meter to each individual room in the house, and comments made on general services such as water, electricity, gas supply and drainage.

Not many people use a surveyor in Spain. They will probably be Spanish and a survey costs around 1,000€ plus additional translation costs. People embarking on a building project normally have enough confidence in their structural knowledge to trust their own judgment and those who don't should not be embarking on such a large project in the first place.

Assuming all these checks are satisfactory it is now safe to purchase the property and proceed to the next step of obtaining a *licencia de obra* (building licence) from the local town hall.

PURCHASING LAND

Before purchasing either urban or rural land a number of vital enquiries have to be made. Most important is the planning status attached to it which may prevent development. For example it may be designated an area of beauty or for a specific purpose only. With areas of outstanding beauty, retaining natural charm is often a key issue with planning departments. Asking planning authorities to change this designation is difficult. On the other hand planning applications are almost automatic where an area has been approved for urbanisation or general housing development.

Urban land

Look for a town plan called the *Plan General de Ordenacion Urbana (PGOU)*, the municipal building plan. Drawing it up involves both local and regional government, with the latter not always approving the usually overambitious plans of the former. It involves political, social and legal considerations. A town plan is not a static document. It can involve strategic planning and detailed consideration of individual planning applications. Looking at a plan is one thing, understanding it is another, more complex issue, with specialist help often necessary.

Rural land

The purchase of rural land has further complications. Where are the boundaries? Are there any rights over the land? What can it be used for? All these factors have to be checked before proceeding. While the boundaries may be marked by paint on rocks, numbers, or metal stakes in the ground, this is useless if a defining piece of paper contradicts these markers.

Lastly where crops and trees are growing, or land is used for agricultural purposes, check the water rights. Check the road access for winter rain. Are there any tracks or rights of way across the land? Are there any building developments or roads planned close by? Will the property be overlooked by any other higher development obstructing the line of sight? Do adjoining neighbours have any prior purchasing rights?

Contracts and checks

Buying land is much the same as buying a house. It needs a contract and an *escritura* and a visit to the notary. It requires the payment of *IVA* which in the case of land is 16 per cent (remember it is only seven per cent for a property). It also requires pre-purchase checks and the one check that nearly always ends in some discussion is about boundaries of rural land since they are often described in vague terms. If problems exist with boundaries an official surveyor *(topografo)* can survey and measure the land thus identifying its boundaries and size. The findings form part of a new *escritura*. Thereafter the way to proceed is to compare the *escritura* (assuming one exists) with the *catastro* certificate (a map with boundaries). There needs to be officially recognised boundaries and a statement of the exact square metres in both documents. While they may not agree initially, this can be corrected upon purchase when a new *escritura* and a new *catastro* description are brought in line.

All done and correct? It is now safe to purchase the land and proceed to the next step of obtaining a *licencia de obra* (building licence) from the local town hall.

BUILDING LICENCE – NEW AND RENOVATED PROPERTIES

Officially titled *licencia de obra* – a building licence – this document can also be called a building permit or *permiso de obra*. It is necessary to have a building licence to build a property on a piece of land in the country or in the town. It is also necessary for renovating an older property.

Previous checks at the town hall will have given an assurance that there is no objection in principle to being issued with a building licence, which is the equivalent of planning permission. When discussions took place the issue of local building codes will have arisen, such as the distance between the boundary and any other building, the distance between a wall and a road, the number of storeys and what about any established urbanisation approval?

You need to understand the applicable building codes before submitting final plans. It may be that approval of building licences can be influenced. A Spaniard accompanied by a local architect and builder known to the town hall planning people will gain maximum flexibility from the codes. Foreigners, who are often accustomed to obtaining planning permission for as little as a garden shed, like to keep to the rules but find the whole planning system wearisome and unless accompanied by a local architect or Spanish solicitor they are unlikely to be able to grapple with the issues involved. To obtain the required building licence, a detailed set of plans with a building specification, called a *memoria,* must be submitted for approval.

Delay often accompanies the final issue of a building licence. It is the point of no return for local authorities. Final approval may be referred to Provincial or *Comunidad* level if the project involves a change from *rustico* to *urbano* designation or the district does not have an approved *Plan General de Ordenacion Urbana (PGOU)*. Building licences come so much quicker when renovating a ruin compared to building new – a ruin is unsightly and in the eyes of the planners best upgraded. Lastly, one person frequently called to assist a private person is the local Mayor. Remember they usually want the project to succeed and, of course, a personal vote.

Do you really need an architect?

There are two main ways to obtain a building plan. One method is to go to a local builder who will have a stock of house types which can be altered to individual requirements. The second method is to have plans drawn up by an independent architect, local or from anywhere in the EU, in line with individual tastes and requirements.

A good architect can match financial limitations to budget, sort out muddled thinking, design a home and steer a project through the planning stages. The best way to find a good architect is by personal recommendation. Find one who has worked on a similar project, where examples of their work can be seen and references obtained.

There is pressure for the appointment of architects. It reduces the number of unsightly designs and removes some responsibility from the town hall to other qualified individuals. In fact architects' drawings are necessary to obtain a building permit and an architect signs off the completed building. The minimum architect's fee is set by their *Colegio de Arquitectos* at six per cent of the estimated construction cost. However, as is the way in Spain, the estimated cost of construction will be reduced by around 20 per cent in all official documents. The actual construction cost will be around 75 per cent of the finished market value. An *aparejador* (building engineer) is the architect's right hand man. They supervise building construction on the architect's behalf with a charge of 1.5 per cent of estimated construction cost.

If it goes wrong

Builders often say 'you can build anything you want here. If it goes wrong we will pay the fine.' Don't believe it! The statement may be accurate, it may be made with the best of intentions, but it is not correct or contractually binding. Some people deliberately build without permission. If the town hall does not object within seven years, it is approved. If permission has not been granted, or an alteration has breached planning rules, a fine of five per cent of the alteration value is imposed, provided the modification is deemed satisfactory and can be legalised. Blatant breeches accrue a fine of 20 per cent and the building is demolished.

Development deals

Along the Mediterranean building is taking place at a prodigious rate. In some popular areas planning authorities have special deals with a developer. Land is re-zoned to permit greater building in exchange for part of a developer's profits going to increase the town's revenue. This does raise a few eyebrows, especially where a mayor or councillors have an interest in the land, but it is not illegal. The best that can be said is the extra income assists all residents in reducing taxes.

BUILDING SPECIFICATION

The architect prepares a *memoria de calidades* (building specification). While many items, such as concrete, bricks and electrical wiring, are standard, many are not: roof tiles, floor tiles, wall tiles; electrical fittings, bathroom fittings and kitchen fittings; doors and windows! Getting the *memoria* correct is important as a builder uses it to prepare a competitive quotation. Any changes or extras made later will cost more, usually a lot more, as they are no longer competing.

A modern Spanish house is built to a high specification with little wood used in its construction. It is a strong property, of concrete and brick, which tends to carry sound easily. Water pipes are set unobtrusively in the walls which may cause problems should they leak. A major feature is a low maintaince finish on both inside and outside walls. Spanish houses are designed to achieve coolness in summer. This requirement is aided by the use of window shutters to block out hot summer sunlight.

If a builder fails to meet a building specification they are accountable in law. The *Ley de Ordenacion de Edificacion* makes a builder legally responsible for ten years for any damage resulting from foundations, load-bearing walls and other structural elements. They are responsible for three years for damage caused by construction material defects, and one year for the external finish. An architect is also responsible for ten years for incorrect instructions and undetected defects in the land such as subsidence.

BUILDERS

The *memoria,* used as a basis for quotation, should also be incorporated into a building contract as a basis for payment. As large a fee as possible should be paid on completion and the smallest fee paid up front. A building contract should be similar in style to a contract for an off plan property with emphasis on what is included, method of payment and giving a definite completion date with penalties for late completion. Like a purchase contract this is a key document, not to be considered lightly, and should be checked first by an *abogado.*

All builders have an insurance policy to cover any liability to the public and their employees. It should also cover the possibility of going bankrupt before completing the property. The number and details of this policy should be stated in the purchase contract but often are not, creating some suspicion that insurance may not have been arranged. Strangely it is small builders who are more likely to go bankrupt as larger builders have bank guarantees and bank managers checking their cash flow. The financial consequences of a builder going bankrupt can be serious but time delays, while an alternative builder is found, cause additional frustration.

The balance of an architect, an *aparejador,* a *memoria* and a building contract all checked by an *abogado* should give total safeguard to anyone going it alone. An alternative to all this is just to let the builders in or to build it yourself. You know exactly what you want, are confident of costs and specification. This is not recommended, but when reforming a town house with little or no external modifications, it is often done.

The perils of shortcuts

Many people think they can take shortcuts. Never mind the rules. Who do they meet? A cowboy, a term usually associated with people who offer services in return for a sum of cash, then either disappear, or carry out such horrendous work that the client ends up spending more to rectify the damage.

In the UK many of these cowboys are named and shamed on television. Trading standards officers investigate and some cowboys are prosecuted for the slipshod work they do, or for overcharging customers. But what about Spain, where there is little effective trading standards control? In almost all the cases, a victim has paid thousands of euros to have building work carried out before realising they are being taken for a ride. They meet with aggression from the people who carried out the work: 'Try and sue me, this is Spain and you won't get anywhere'.

In a lot of cases, people prefer to put the experience down to bad luck rather than pursue the matter through the courts. In some cases they realise they have appointed a builder without due care and attention. Very few pursue the matter through the courts, partly through embarrassment and because of the possibility of throwing good money after bad.

To avoid this go by the rules, but if absolutely determined to appoint a builder for a small job, check the credentials of the person being considered. If they are a registered builder then they will be able to show valid *IVA* documentation. Secondly, any good builder will show work they have previously done and allow an independent conversation with their clients so that their credentials are verified. Beware of hidden extras because there should not be any. If changes take place to a specification they should be by mutual agreement and be included on an amendment sheet to the contract. Lastly, at no time pay large cash sums of money up front.

FINAL STEPS

Once the building is complete we are back to the procedures outlined in Chapter 6 Purchasing a Property, starting with the *Certificado Final de la Direccion de la Obra* and the *Licencia de Primera Ocupacion* through to the notary and the *escritura*.

CHARGES AND BUILDING COSTS

Fees and legal costs

Land survey	0.5%
Architect's fee	6.0% (calculated on an artificially low building cost)
Building engineer	1.5% (calculated on an artificially low building cost)
Building licence	2.0% (4.0% of material cost)
Legal costs, including *IVA*	10% to 19% (remember *IVA* on land purchase is 16%)
TOTAL	20% to 29.0%

Building costs

A good specification of construction, for a restored property	750€ per square metre
A good specification of construction, for a new detached property	1,500€ per square metre

Payments to a builder

20% on signing the contract

20% on completion of walls and roof

20% on completion of inside

10% for outside work – walls, patio, pool

10% retained for up to one year to cover snagging defects

IVA – paid on completion or in stages

FURTHER READING

Alex and Erna Fry, *Finca: Renovating an Old Farmhouse in Spain*. Malaga: Santana Ediciones.

9
Selling a Property

INTRODUCTION

While selling procedures are obviously the reverse of buying procedures, there are some things to look out for. Firstly property owners should be aware at the outset that they are subject to capital gains tax on the profits from their sale, whether they are resident or non-resident. Secondly if a property is bought from a non-resident, then five per cent of the purchase price declared in the *escritura* must be deposited with the tax office in the vendor's name. In other words only 95 per cent is paid directly to the vendor. Why? This deposit is designed to cover a non-resident's liability for capital gains tax.

This chapter also covers compulsory purchase – a forced sale – and includes the controversial land grab law called Valencia's *Ley Reguladora de Actividad Urbanística.*

ASSEMBLING THE DOCUMENTS

The first step in selling a property is to assemble copies of all necessary documents. They need to identify the property, the person selling the property and proof that there are no debts or encumbrances on it. Creating a document file gives an

106

impression that a seller knows what they are doing in the eyes of estate agents and buyers.

The most important paper is obviously a copy of the *escritura* which shows the registered owner with an incontestable title. It may well be that a *copia simple* will suffice. If the *escritura* has been lost another copy can be obtained from the notary where it is on file permanently. A prospective purchaser will no doubt obtain a *nota simple* at the *Registro de la Propiedad* which will confirm information in the *escritura*.

Next assemble some personal identification. A copy of a passport or *residencia* will do, but also include a copy of the *certificado de empadronamiento* issued by the town hall which will show names of the people residing at the property.

Include in the information pack an *IBI* receipt for the paid-up *Impuesto Sobre Bienes Inmuebles*, the local tax. This receipt will show the *Valor Catastral,* the official assessed value of the property for tax purposes. This value is almost always less than the real market value. The *IBI* receipt confirms the house exists, is registered for taxes and states the *referencia catastral* number which is required at the notary.

The notary and the Property Registry are concerned with ownership, loans and mortgages while the *Certificado Catastral* is concerned about a property's measurement, boundaries and physical characteristics. So if selling a *finca* (a country house surrounded by land), include a *Certificado Catastral* in the documentation so it is absolutely clear what is on offer.

Present copies of bills for water and electricity. Any buyer will want to be sure there are no debts. For a property within a Community of Property Owners include details of the quota, the yearly charge and a copy of the statutes.

Lastly, is the house being sold furnished? Many Spaniards expect to purchase and sell houses furnished or part furnished. Ex-pats going back home do the same to avoid shipping costs. So to avoid any ambiguity include a furniture inventory even if it just says 'No contents included'.

APPOINTING AN ESTATE AGENT

It is probably better to use an estate agent to sell a property than to go it alone. This is not a decision people feel happy about, because estate agents charge such high commissions. It is an expensive decision but it is often better to bite the bullet and, since Spanish estate agents rarely demand the exclusive right to market a property, a seller should list it with several agents. Each agent will have a different type of agreement in which the commission or reserve price is stated if they bring a client who eventually buys the property. A good estate agent will nurse a sale through the entire process of finding a buyer, negotiating the price, drawing up a contract with an *abogado*, securing payment, signing before a notary, ensuring all necessary taxes and fees are paid and that utility services are transferred to the new owner.

Commission

Agents dealing in Spanish property do take a high commission. The lowest start at around three per cent but the average is ten per cent. When selling a *finca* it can be 25 per cent. How do they justify such exorbitant charges? Their answer is ambiguous, making reference to high advertising costs, commissions due in two countries and complex transactions involving different nationalities. In truth it is simply a seller's market with demand outstripping supply, causing many people to enter the lucrative business of house selling. The commission structure operating for second-hand property, commonly termed a resale property, is as follows:

- the agent asks the seller what price they want for the property;

- they advertise and negotiate a sale of the property at another, higher price;

- the difference between the two prices is the agent's commission.

In the final stages of house price negotiation, an agent's commission itself may well be reviewed downwards. As it is quite common to find several agents selling the same property, and since their commissions may differ, so ironically may the price of the property.

Tricks of the trade

Given the commission structure, an obvious trick is for an agent to convince an owner that the value of a property is, say, 20 per cent less than the market value. An agreement is drawn up between the seller and agent stating they will achieve this price for the owner. If they do, then in addition to a normal ten per cent commission, an extra ten per cent is pocketed. The basic trick can be embellished if it is a distress sale, or in particular if the agent has a power of attorney. The agent has done nothing illegal; after all, the seller signed the agreement. Sharp agents, absent and ignorant owners can lead to stories such as this.

A second trick is to process the sale by an Option Contract which is drawn up by an agent rather than the normal Private Contract drawn up by an *abogado*. Such contracts are distinguished by what is missed out rather than what is stated. They are open to abuse.

Do not forget the favourite trick of the deposit being a cash payment going straight to the agent – effectively black money commission. Where this takes place a normal *factura* (bill) will not be forthcoming from an agent listing the amount of the commission and *IVA*. This is unfortunate, as the entire amount is deductible as a legitimate expense upon calculating capital gains tax liability.

SELLING PROCEDURE

A seller and buyer, with the assistance of an agent, will agree details of a purchase. A Private Contract is drawn up by an *abogado,* at which time the buyer makes a substantial non-returnable deposit. This deposit holds the property for the buyer until an agreed date at which time the buyer pays the full purchase price, either from their own resources or by obtaining a *hipoteca* (mortgage). If the buyer does not complete the sale, they lose the deposit. If for whatever reason the seller does not complete the sale, double the amount of the deposit is returned to the buyer. The two parties complete the transaction at the notary and sign the *escritura* when the balance of money exchanges hands.

While selling a property is simply the reverse of buying one, some key issues need to be addressed:

- the division of costs associated with a property transfer;

- the value to be put in the *escritura* ;

- the role of an *abogado.*

Plus Valia Tax

Remember the comments in Chapter 7: 'Of course it is the seller who should pay this tax. They have gained the benefit of the increase in land value. The law of the country supports this view. In practice however this tax has often fallen on the purchaser since it a more secure method of collection. After all, a vendor may flee the country leaving this tax unpaid.'

Who pays the *Plus Valia* tax? The normal practice of this being to the account of the buyer needs to be confirmed.

Value in the *escritura*

Again remember the comments in Chapter 7 where it was stated that it is quite common to have two purchase prices for a property. One price is the actual price paid exclusive of any fees or taxes. The other is a lower price declared in the *escritura*. 'All taxes and fees are calculated on the value stated in the *escritura*, not the actual price paid. The Transfer Tax or *IVA* charged at seven per cent is effectually reduced to 5.6 per cent if the *escritura* value is declared at 80 per cent of the market value.'

The purchaser may wish to declare the full purchase price, or no less than 80 per cent of the purchase price, in the *escritura*. The seller will wish to have 80 per cent of the purchase price declared to reduce any capital gains tax liability. Of course the seller's position will be influenced by any substantial under-declaration on their part when initially purchasing the property.

How is this resolved? The seller can perform a number of calculations to determine the least damaging position, but to coin a phrase 'at the end of the day it is the buyer who calls the shots'. If the buyer wants 80 per cent or 100 per cent, or any other figure in between, declared in the *escritura* then that is what happens. Why? The buyer has the legal right to do so.

Role of an *abogado*

Let us again remind ourselves of some of the comments in Chapter 6. 'It is not necessary in Spain to have two *abogados*. It is accepted that only one is necessary, as a contract drawn up by an *abogado* can be assumed to be correct. After all the final legal safeguard, the notary, is still to come. An agent selling a property normally appoints an *abogado*. The contract may be perfectly legal but it is possible it will contain clauses more favourable to the seller than the buyer. But who pays the bill? The buyer. It is wise for the buyer to appoint an *abogado* to draw up a contract or to take other additional independent legal advice prior to signing a contract.'

Conventional wisdom states a buyer may need two *abogados* but a seller certainty will not.

CAPITAL GAINS TAX

Exemption

Details of how to calculate CGT are contained in Chapter 14 on personal taxation. There is exemption if:

* the property was bought before 1987;

* the owner is 65 years old, a resident, and has lived in the property for a minimum of three years;

* the owner is a resident using the full purchase price to buy another principal residence in Spain.

Buying from a non-resident

Anyone buying a property from a non-resident is required to subtract five per cent from the purchase price and pay it to the tax office within 30 days of the transaction. This is a deposit against a vendor trying to avoid paying capital gains tax. Provided the buyer deducts five per cent from the purchase price they cannot be pursued for additional CGT if the seller's liability was greater than five per cent and they fail to pay it. However, if the buyer fails to subtract and pay five per cent tax, they are liable to pay all CGT due on the sale.

After paying five per cent, a buyer must give the vendor a copy of the completed tax form. The vendor must then apply for a return of the difference between the five per cent deposit and total CGT liability. However this is an unlikely scenario, as a non-resident's liability to CGT is probably more than five per cent of the sale price.

COMPULSORY PURCHASE

Having a local authority purchase a property or piece of land can hardly be regarded as a sale. There is however a requirement for them to pay a fair price and go through a judicial process. The system is known as expropriation (to take away, or transfer from an owner, for public use). For most people, any improvement in public services such as a new road is good news but not necessarily so if it affects an individual.

The authorities are represented by the public works department, *Ministerio de Obras Públicas y Transportes,* which informs the owner that expropriation proceedings are about to begin by sending a letter inviting those affected to attend a hearing in the town hall. Once the extent of expropriation is defined, the authorities communicate an offer of payment which if acceptable concludes the matter. But it is the degree of expropriation that is often the issue. Where there are different ideas on a small piece of land, a building or even part of a building, discussions on value are often necessary. Expert advice too is taken.

Unable to come to an agreement with the authorities? Then go to the *Jurado de Expropiaciones,* a special court set up for this purpose. Its members comprise not only judges but property experts too and its decisions have ensured that a fair market value has been paid to many property and land owners. However it must be stated that the chances of resisting expropriation are not good, because in law public benefit always takes precedence over private ownership.

Compare the fairness of this system with the so termed 'land grab' approach of the Valencian *Comunidad* below.

Valencia's *Ley Reguladora de Actividad Urbanistica*

Property owners in the Valencian Autonomous Community should be aware that under the Valencian Government's *Ley Reguladora de la Actividad Urbanistica* of 1994, all land may be converted for property development, unless it has been deemed *no urbanizable* on historical, cultural or ecological grounds.

This means that even *rustico* (rural land) may be redesignated as fit for property development if the town hall approves a developer's plan for such a change in use. Land classed as *urbanizable* is also, by definition, appropriate for development. It is therefore important when buying property in the Comunidad of Valencia, which includes the Costa Blanca, to check future development plans at the local town hall. This is also advisable even where land is already deemed to be *urbano,* since only by checking the status of a property can one become aware of the implications of likely future developments.

The Valencian regional law regulating urban development was passed with the aim of stimulating urban development. Many parts of the region were caught in a situation where normal urban growth was paralysed by a maze of smallholdings whose owners refused to sell or to participate in development projects. Town planners found their projects blocked by stubborn people. As a result the rationalisation of streets, sewage, lighting systems and parks required for harmonious urban growth could not go ahead.

To deal with this situation, the regional government came up with new rules. The legislation provides for compulsory participation by landowners in development projects backed by town halls, and ensures that existing owners do not benefit from windfall profits. These profits occur when an owner in the path of development discovers their formerly rural farm is about to become a city block. The land is suddenly worth a fortune. Paying for this formerly fell to other taxpayers. So the

Valencian authorities designed a way to make the landowners pay their share.

The town hall plan and carry out an urbanisation project on their own, or designate a private developer as an 'urbanising agent'. The latter is the most common. This delegated private developer then acts as an agent of the municipal authority, with the right to take private land or compel payment for it even when the owner does not wish to sell.

If planning is approved

Owners of property where a change of classification is approved receive a notice from the town hall that they have 15 days in which to comment on the proposed new use. They may argue to preserve the *status quo* or in some way to protect their existing rights, but as matters stand the probability is that the change of use will be permitted, perhaps with some modification. The town hall's decision is subject to approval by the Valencian Government.

If planning is approved, current owners will be obliged to contribute to the new development. This may involve having some of their land expropriated for compensation, which will depend on the existing classification of the land. Owners may also have to make a financial contribution to the construction of roads, drains, lighting and other urban development costs.

This is clearly not what the law was designed for. In fact there is a major loophole in it. Through protests and publicity there is a determination to make the authorities in Valencia, Madrid, London and Brussels aware of the injustice of this system and to demand a change, but the Valencia authorities seem slow to react. This will happen sometime because the present situation is intolerable. Until then ... beware when purchasing property in the Comunidad of Valencia.

LAND GRAB – A TYPICAL CASE STUDY

This is a story of my house in the sun. It's not a big villa but that's irrelevant. It's been our family home for 20 years and my husband and I worked very hard to pay for it, just the same as everyone else. I came to Spain almost 30 years ago, when I was a teenager, met my husband, a local Spaniard, within a couple of hours of getting off the coach. We lived 'happily ever after' until two years ago when a nightmare descended upon us.

An acquaintance of ours, who has known my husband all his life, inherited his father's extensive orange groves and before the old man was cold in his grave he and his associates got hold of more land and put forward a *plan parcial* to the town hall, which was duly accepted.

We had one letter from their lawyers in 2002. I duly went to the town hall planning department, was told that I would lose 50 per cent of my land to the developers and ten per cent to the council and would have to pay my share of infrastructure improvement costs, whatever they amounted to.

In 2004 our neighbour received a letter from the developers regarding a meeting and as we had both engaged the same lawyer, he represented us. The developers claimed we only had 700 square metres of land and in a second meeting would inform us how the sector would be broken into plots and where the urbanisation roads would go.

We're now in the situation where the *plan parcial* has been finally approved and published on the Official Provincial Bulletin website. It gave us a period of 20 days to decide if we wanted to pay our share of the development or whether we would concede more land. It was our lawyer who finally explained the issue. We lose 60 per cent of our garden; this may or may not include the house, we don't know yet. We have scraped up the hefty sum of 90,000€ which has been deposited with our bank so we can guarantee the sum whenever the developers request it. Our lawyer has officially notified both the town hall and the developer, but failing this we will have a further 500 square metres of our land automatically taken away.

We will be left with less than 600 square metres and, hopefully, the house; but this is under the size of the minimum plot required to build in the zone which the town hall has reclassified to 800 square metres. We did have 1,300 originally. Our lawyer tells us we can't actually remain on the smaller plot. We have an option of buying back the 200 square metres necessary to take the plot to the minimum required, but this will be at market price.

Some advice

This story will roll on. It is familiar to people in the Valencian region who have a property close to rural or undeveloped land. What can be done about it?

The best thing is to find a lawyer who does not carry out work for a local council and who specialises in urban law. They will at least be able to understand the bureaucratic process, which can last for years. There will be several steps that will have to be taken within short time limits and an owner may not be aware or properly informed of these. Non-compliance with these requests, or failure to officially notify an answer in a stipulated time, may make things worse.

The first, and possibly only, notification received will be in the *BOP* Valencian bulletin, which can be accessed over the web, plus a notice in a local (Spanish) newspaper. Of course one can go to the town hall for information and even though they may appear helpful, they can be misleading, withholding information unless specifically requested. Even then an expert is required to explain exactly what these documents signify.

Hundreds of people have banded together and joined the *AUN* association (*Abusos Urbanisticos No*), for mutual support and advice. Residents of all nationalities and age groups are presenting a united front. Contact details: www.abusos-no.org

10

Community of Property Owners

INTRODUCTION

A Community of Property Owners is a mechanism of self-regulation common in continental Europe and in the USA but unusual in the UK except in up-market apartments. When a number of people own land or buildings in such a way that they have exclusive use of part of the property, but a shared use in the remainder, a *comunidad* is created.

In a *comunidad* the owner holds the house or apartment outright and shares the use of the remaining areas as part of a community of owners. It is not only a shared pool or TV aerial that is jointly owned but any lift shafts, common corridors, entrances and parking areas. While members of the *comunidad* are each responsible for their own home, they collectively agree the action required upon those common areas and become responsible for paying their share of common expenses.

The community is managed by an elected committee which appoints a president and secretary, both of whom are residents in the community. Day to day management can be delegated to a professional administrator, who need not be a resident in the community.

HOW IT WORKS

The community of property owners (*comunidad de propietarios*) is regulated by the Law of Horizontal Property (*La Ley de Propiedad Horizontal*) which was passed in 1960 and amended in 1999. Some urbanisations of detached villas do not come under the Horizontal Law as roads, drains and lighting may serve the public as well as residents, thus requiring collaboration between owners and the town hall. One of the provisions of the 1999 amendment makes it easier for them to use the protection of the Horizontal Law.

A property contract, the *escritura* and the law surrounding communities binds an owner to the actual community regulations.

A property owner requires no more than an understanding of the legal principles. There are many English language translations and interpretations of the law itself, suitable for those who seek appointment as president or a committee member. For the president in particular, the only legally appointed person, a full understanding of procedural issues is necessary for there are many minority groups seeking to trip up the unwary.

Common areas

When the word urbanisation is mentioned it will always mean a community of property owners. It is by far the most common form of property ownership for foreign buyers in Spain. In an urbanisation the communal areas can include roads, gardens, swimming pools, communal satellite TV systems and possibly, in composite developments, a small marina or golf area. The common areas in an apartment block are the lifts, lobby, stairs, foundations and the roof. Any property that shares facilities will automatically become a member of the relevant *comunidad*. Fully detached villas, *fincas* and town houses in a public street have no shared facilities and therefore do not form part of any community.

Registration

Each *comunidad* is registered at the local property registry for each town, with a set of statutes defining common areas. By law it should also hold at least one general meeting of all residents each year, and elect one of its members as its president and one as secretary, both assisted by a committee. Large communities will have a more complex structure, often employing a professional administrator to carry out management of the urbanisation. In mainly foreign-owned urbanisations this role is often taken on by a development company or an administrator first appointed by the developers on behalf of the community.

Administrador de fincas

This is a licensed property administrator belonging to a *Colegio* who handles property matters such as paying property taxes, managing rentals and ensuring records are properly kept. An *administrador de finca* is employed by property owners to ensure the community's affairs are handled professionally. They may manage several communities, may be part of an estate agency or even a subsidiary of a developer.

Purpose

The role of the committee is to ensure that common parts are maintained, set the community charges, agree a written set of rules and oversee spending. It has to be said however that it is often difficult to establish these principles in the minds of residents, who often see the committee as a complaints board. The rules set by the *comunidad* are intended to improve the quality of life of residents. They usually deal with concerns about noise, the pool, pets and the overall standard of the urbanisation or apartment.

Quota

The quota is the percentage of total community costs and voting rights allocated to a particular property. Since all properties are not exactly the same size the amount paid will vary, the exact percentage being stated in the *escritura*. The overall community spending plan is set at each year's AGM. The net effect of quotas and actual spending can be seen in a property owner's annual bill, although in a new urbanisation this is not available for two years.

Meetings

As befits a Spanish regulation, indeed a self-regulating law requiring voluntary agreement between people, procedural issues dominate. The AGM can be entertaining or frustrating. It can be like a bullfight. All human frailties are on display. Not only do you get to know your neighbour quickly but the quirks of their mind too. As fully trained administrators the Spanish love it. The Germans seek order. The laid back Scandinavians give it a miss and the Brits cannot cope with it at all. On display are people who love being on committees, those who question every euro spent and those who are simply belligerent. When problems arise it is because of money – where some residents wish to take on an extra expense and some do not. A communal swimming pool is a fruitful topic of conversation. So too is noise. Discussion on items can be made worse where urbanisations have an ongoing history of bad relationships, where different nationalities cannot work together, or the views of residents and non-residents are irreconcilable.

A minute book of the last annual general meeting will demonstrate any problems. An agenda, minutes of meetings, a list of owners' names with their allocated quotas, updated payments or debts, are all published for every meeting. The meetings are formal and often long but 'find a friend' as proxy voting is allowed.

FURTHER READING

David Searl, *You and the Law in Spain*. Malaga: Santana Ediciones. A translation of the actual law, together with an interpretation and guidance. Very useful for community presidents.

11

Letting and Ownership Schemes

INTRODUCTION

Spain has had its problems with letting laws. Under laws from 1964 to 1985 tenants were so protected that landlords 'threw in the towel', leading to a critical housing shortage. This old law protected tenants so strongly that they could pass on their rights to children and grandchildren. Rent could never be raised, or only by a fraction of the inflation rate. Tenants refused to vacate and were entitled to an extension of their contract, regardless of the landlord's desire to end a letting. Landlords often left their apartments empty rather than risk having sitting tenant problems and refused to repair buildings.

Recent legislation

Of course things had to change and revised rental laws were passed in 1985 aimed at rectifying this situation. The new law provided all contracts ended when they said they would without provision for a forcible extension. The law also ended any restrictions on rent increases. So the pendulum swung! Rents began to rise and short-term contracts, with little protection for the tenant, were offered. Now it was the tenants who suffered.

Enter the last piece of legalisation. The 1995 law called the *Ley de Arrendamientos* was designed to provide a better balance between the rights and needs of tenants and landlords and to bring a final solution to the generations of sitting tenants under the 1964/85 laws that all but ruined the rental market. The law ends the forcible extension of rental contracts by the tenant, allows a landlord to raise the old low rents and to recover their own property. It provides tenants with more security than the 1985 law, obliging landlords to renew residential rental contracts for up to five years. It also establishes a landlord's right to a deposit of one month's rent for an unfurnished property and two months' rent for a furnished property as a guarantee against damages.

This chapter also looks at other ownership schemes as an alternative to rental. They fall somewhere in between purchase and rental. Miss-sold timeshares, imaginative low-cost leasebacks and co-ownership schemes complete a varied picture of property ownership.

RENTAL OWNERS

While the situation differs in large cities, in coastal areas the vast majority of available lettings are from people who have bought homes according to their needs for size, price and location. They have bought holiday homes and are not so much looking to make a profit from renting, as hoping to cover some or all of the costs of purchase, through rental income, by letting them casually to family and friends. They are holiday homes for their own use, with owners ready to compromise on business issues, thus reducing potential income, in order to maximise their own enjoyment.

A smaller number of people see property exclusively as an investment and want to rent on a serious basis. They want to make money by letting their property and will try to find the maximum number of tenants each year. Decisions taken about where and what to buy, and what facilities to provide, will be governed by a wish to maximise profit. They put themselves in the position of a person who may wish to rent their property and consider which part of the market they expect to appeal to: whether it is couples wanting to enjoy rural Spain or families wanting a traditional beach holiday, or groups on a golfing break. They choose an area, a location, buy a property and equip it solely with their prospective tenants in mind.

Lastly there is a breed of people who 'Buy to Let' for fun and profit. They seek a balance between casual letting and serious letting. They want to enjoy the property and make money too!

WHAT MAKES A GOOD RENTAL PROPERTY?

Travelling time

Travel industry figures state that about 25 per cent of all potential visitors to Spain will be deterred if it involves travelling for more than one hour from an airport at either end of their journey, and if that time rises to one and a half hours it will deter around 50 per cent. This may well mean firstly that some people never leave home and secondly Spanish rural cottages are difficult to let. But the key criterion for renting is that the closer to a Spanish airport the easer it is to find tenants.

Facilities

A holiday rental property should be located as close as possible to main attractions such as a beach and shopping facilities. For some tenants the proximity to a historic town or the countryside would be a major asset, while for others it might be nightlife that is the main attraction.

Having a property located close to activities such as golf, sailing, tennis and hiking can achieve rental income outside the high season. A property near to a golf course will not only have excellent views and lush greenery, but golfers keep on coming all year round. A bonus of many golf courses is that they are near to a beautiful coast thus providing a double tenant market.

Convenience

Holiday tenants do not want to cook all the time. They want to eat out. A property will be much easier to let if it is within easy walking distance of bars and restaurants.

A swimming pool is necessary in some areas, as properties with pools are much easier to let than those without. Some private letting agencies will not handle properties without a pool.

Owners' possessions

One difficult judgment is deciding the contents and a standard of furnishing for each rental property. It can be argued that any standard of furnishing is permissible provided somebody is willing to pay the rent. But letting through an agency, a holiday company or a Tourist Board, or positioning the letting up market, means certain minimum standards must be met.

For a property to be attractive to paying tenants, the furniture and fittings should be comfortable and of good quality. The three most common complaints about holiday lettings are uncomfortable beds, poor quality and lack of the kitchen equipment and lack of easy chairs.

A rental which is occupied by the owner should not have too many personal items lying around as personal possessions tend to clutter up properties, so tenants have nowhere to put their own bits and pieces. Tenants actually want a rental to look similar to a hotel room – clean, bland, no clutter, sterile and no personal traces of the owner which means, ironically, that when the owner occupies the property, they have to live like a tenant.

CHOOSING LETTING AGENTS

The advantage of using a letting agency is that they put some distance between the owner and the tenant, they handle references, inventories, deposits, and direct debits and they can intervene if disputes arise. No spare time? Then use an agent, who will take care of everything, and save the time and expense of advertising and finding clients. It also makes sense to use an agency if the owner lives a long way from the property, in say the UK, or if it is a specialised property likely to command a high rental.

No agent can magically produce a tenant. Agencies can do their best, but they cannot create tenants where a market does not exist. They cannot guarantee that there will be no void periods, or that the property will be let for 365 days of the year. If an owner finds tenants for holiday letting then all the paid rent is retained, but using a letting agency will cost at least 12.5 per cent if not more, of the agreed rental in commission. These charges rise when increased services are offered.

Always choose a letting agent with care. They should have a separate client account that cannot be raided to keep their business going. Use a specialist letting agency, rather than an estate agent who has a letting business as a sideline. Where lettings are their only concern, they have to work harder otherwise they have no business.

The agreement between the owner and a letting agent or even a tour operator is called a *Contrato de Encargo de Appensmiento* (Contract of Letting). It is normally written in Spanish with an English translation.

LETTING CONTRACTS

Holiday contracts

A holiday tenant renting a property from a company or person in say England, France or Germany will have a contract written in the language of that country, signed before leaving on vacation. This is perfectly acceptable. The contract should make provision for terms and conditions associated with a holiday letting, covering statements on the following:

- Payments: it is usual to request a deposit to secure a booking – usually a percentage paid in advance, with the balance payable at some specified date before arrival.

- Cancellation: people should be encouraged to take out holiday cancellation insurance.

- Policy statements on who are not welcome, for example children, pets and single-sex groups.

- Bed linen, table linen, towels – provision and charging.

- Facilities for children, cots, highchairs and fireguards.

- Smoking policy.

- Guests' responsibility for their own belongings and cars.

- Arrival and departure times.

- Breakages and damages policy.

Temporada contracts

Short-term contracts are called *Arrienda de Temporada*. A straightforward, standard contract is written in Spanish and normally in the native tongue of the tenant. It is for a period of up to one year although most are for much less than that. Properties let this way are furnished and the contract should include a detailed inventory of contents with a returnable deposit required to cover any damages caused by the temporary tenant. The contract is for a specific period of time at a stated price. The renewal of the contract is only at the agent's or landlord's discretion. A standard contract is available from some *tabacs* (state owned tobacco shop that additionally hold a supply of stamps and stationery forms).

Vivienda contracts

A contract for a long-term rental is called *Arrienda de Vivienda*. The law provides for long-term rentals to be of up to five years' duration, thus giving the tenant a degree of security. If a landlord offers a contract of three years' duration, which is accepted, and then the tenant wishes to stay on for another two years, it is automatically renewed on the same terms. If the tenant leaves after three years as arranged, then the contract is terminated. Annual rent increases, in line with inflation, take place during the contracted term. A new level of rent is set at the commencement of a new contract. At the end of a five-year *Vivienda* contract the landlord is obliged to notify the tenant officially by a notarised letter, well before the end of the period. If the landlord does not notify the tenant officially, the contract can be renewed for two years at the same rent.

Which contract?

It is important to determine at the outset if a holiday letting contract, short-term letting or long-term letting is being asked, or offered. Legal advisors in Spain struggle to write individual *Vivienda* contracts because of their complexity and the need to cover every eventuality. They often advise the issue of successive *Temporada* contracts for a letting of more than one year, thus bypassing some tenant rights. In this case the lawyer is taking advantage of the tenant, denying them the right to a longer contract, and leaving the way open for rent increases beyond the level of inflation at the end of the year. Some tenants simply accept this practice, but others get legal advice and go to court. The tenant declares they signed a one-year *Temporada* contract, that he or she lives and works there, it is home, and perhaps says they signed a one-year contract under duress and ask the court to order the contract to be extended to the full five years. In many cases the court has ruled in favour of the tenant.

The law lays down the basic structure of rental contracts but they can vary in detail. It is important to make sure everything is understood prior to offering or signing a *Temporada* or *Vivienda* contract. Community charges and local taxes are the responsibility of the owner and an allowance for this may be included in the rent but not added as an extra. No matter the length of time a property is let it is the landlord who is a member of any *Comunidad* (the owner of a community property with shared common elements).

OBEYING THE RULES

The regulation of tourist accommodation is a matter for each *Comunidad*. This means tourist accommodation laws vary throughout Spain, with island hot spots on the receiving end of a number of directives. It is perfectly proper for the Spanish authorities to regulate accommodation in this manner, ensuring that visitors are not overcharged and facilities are of a recognised standard.

Registration

As an example, the Valencia government asks that owners register their accommodation with the Tourist Board. It may be in the city, a metropolitan area or in the country. It may be a simple property let out for a few weeks a year, a bed and breakfast, a guesthouse or a hotel. Either way it has to be registered if utilised for one day or 52 weeks per year. Over one year, which of course in letting terms is a *Vivienda* contract, free market forces apply with no registration necessary.

Registering letting accommodation appears to offer the owner few advantages since a copy of the ten-page application goes to the tax authorities. As a consequence, people conveniently ignore it. For a property in a city, or an upmarket villa on the coast available for a few weeks a year, this may be an acceptable risk. One advantage of having a property listed at the Tourist Office is local marketing assistance, but in many cases it is an inappropriate tool as clients will come from the UK. Since these properties are unlikely to infringe any minimum standard, policing from the Tourist Board too is a waste of their time. So registration is ignored by both parties. A registered property does however carry greater legal protection in the event of a dispute.

Renting out a property as holiday accommodation throughout the year and providing similar services to a hotel such as bed and breakfast means the property must be registered. It is now a business! This means that inspectors will be obliged to come and carry out an assessment of standards, including food preparation. There is another important distinction. A small investor will have the revenue from letting taxed in the normal way as income, but a business with a significant turnover is an altogether different matter.

Letting

It is necessary to check that letting is permitted under any community rules. Additional regulations apply in the Balearics and Canary Islands where letting is not encouraged. You also need to notify the insurance company.

Selling the property

If the landlord sells a property, they are required by law to offer it first to any long-term tenant. It is similar to the sale of rustic land which should be offered first to adjacent land owners. If a landlord sells the property without informing the tenant in advance, the tenant has the right to have this sale annulled.

Tax

Non-residents are liable for Spanish income tax of 25 per cent on all rental income even if a tenant pays in a different currency before leaving for Spain. Legally income arises in Spain because the property is in Spain. Owners letting their property occasionally for a few weeks a year may say nothing about this to the tax authorities and their chances of getting caught are slim. Nevertheless tax is due on any income arising in Spain. Residents on the other hand can reduce rental income by 50 per cent for tax purposes when submitting their annual tax return.

EVICTION AND COMPLAINTS

Eviction

Under what conditions can an owner regain their property and evict a tenant? Failure to pay the rent, damage to the property, using the property for immoral purposes, subletting unless agreed in the contract and causing a serious nuisance to the neighbours are some obvious reasons.

Assuming the contract and law states a rental period is finished, a landlord will also have difficulty evicting someone who chooses to stay. Common abuse takes place with holiday rentals where tenants have signed up for one month and then simply remained in the property without paying any further rent.

In all cases a court order must be obtained against the tenant. Six months later, a landlord is able to obtain an eviction order, but the tenants have lived rent-free for that period. The court will issue a judgment against them for the amount of rent owed, but by then they will have simply moved on. Spanish landlords are reluctant to go to court due to this delay and often take matters into their own hands by forcefully evicting a tenant.

Complaints

Occasionally a landlord may have to deal with a complaint from a tenant. Acknowledge, investigate, make a decision, reply and take remedial action if applicable. If it is valid put matters right, informing the tenant and giving an expected timescale. Otherwise, state no action is required and give the reasons. Complaints may come from sources other than a tenant. In fact they may be about the tenants.

A tenant of a property can also complain to a Tourist Office in the province or town where the property is located, provided the property has been registered in the first place. The Tourist Office will often side with the landlord provided all the necessary procedures have been adhered to. Complaints from longer-term tenants are usually addressed to the *Oficina Municipal de Informacion al Consumidor* (see Chapter 12) which is the consumer information office, directed by regional government to deal with consumer problems such as rents.

BUSINESS IS BUSINESS

Renting property is not democracy in action. It is a business. It is important for an owner to strike the right tone in a relationship with a tenant or letting agent. It should not be arbitrary or dictatorial. The customer may always be correct but the owner has to be in charge and how the tenant, agent or tour operator is handled will largely determine what happens to a property.

The owner sets the tone. The tone may vary depending on the tenant market. If the business is well run, it will be because the owner knows how to run it smoothly and how to communicate, giving a clear set of guidelines and expectations. Let people know what is to be done for them as a landlord and what is expected of them in return.

What tenants are told about a property is part of an education programme. Some landlords want their tenants to know that they are dealing with a large, powerful concern. In some cases the landlords do not even want the tenant to know who the owners are. They prefer to have the tenants think they are dealing with a management company. This way there is an organised management programme and the tenants have to fit into it. Everyone gets treated the same way. Other landlords want their clients to know they are dealing with a friendly individual who will look after all their needs at the drop of a hat, particularly if they are paying top dollar for a luxury villa with a pool in the summer season.

Setting the tone in any business involves dealing with people. Property problems are almost invariably people problems. Apartments do not break their own windows or doors. Buildings do not draw on the walls, or put holes in the carpets. Tenants do not do this, either, unless they think that they can get away with it. Properties do not cause problems. Buildings just sit there, quietly minding their own business. Sure, houses and other types of property are quite capable of producing anxiety. Roofs leak, sewer and other pipe lines break, paint wears off and lawns need periodic cutting. Then there are fires, floods, blizzards, earthquakes, tornadoes, hurricanes and all the other possible calamities beyond the property owner's control. But tenants are the main source of problems that an owner will encounter.

TIMESHARE

Timeshares still remain a popular method of gaining access to a holiday property. You simply buy the right to occupy a property for a set period each year – usually just two weeks. One attraction is the lack of responsibility of home ownership as maintenance and so on is delegated to a management company for an annual fee. Timeshares are most frequently available in big developments, apartment and resort complexes.

The main principal of timeshare is that it gives a quality accommodation for less than the equivalent hotel rate. Their popularity remains high in spite of the fact that timeshares are notorious for scams and rip-offs. Because of their poor reputation other names are now used for these schemes, such as 'vacation ownership' or 'holiday ownership' or such like, but the basic concept is still the same. Nearly all the problems associated with timeshares arise from the way they are sold. Touts go around buttonholing tourists on every street corner. Show some interest? Then an immediate presentation (intensive sales pitch) at an up-market club (windowless prison with no escape) with a meal (cheap red wine) takes place. Freedom is obtained by immediately signing up for a timeshare and paying a vastly 'reduced' deposit with a credit card.

One reason for it being an industry with a bad reputation for miss-selling is its vague legal status somewhere between ownership and renting. This is changing. Spain and most of Europe introduced new timeshare regulations in 1999. The highlights are:

• Restrictions on high pressure selling tactics in public places and tourist spots.

- Introducing a cooling off period of ten days during which the buyer can withdraw from the contract with no penalty.

- Written information to be supplied in the mother tongue of the buyer.

- Contract disputes governed by local law.

In the UK the product is now regulated by the Financial Services Act which means clients obtain protection and are able to sue their financial advisor if they believe they have been given inappropriate advice.

Value for money?

The average timeshare buyer is a well educated home owner, with two cars and no children, who takes at least two holidays and two short breaks per year. The average price for a timeshare is about 12,000 euros for an apartment sleeping four for a purchase period of 20 to 99 years.

Timeshares are poor value for money. The major attraction is low upfront costs but set against the actual value of the property it is around 12 per cent for a two-week period. A developer selling 26 such slots will make 200 per cent profit, less marketing overheads. On top of this there are management fees, the equivalent of community charges in an urbanisation, but without an owner's control of costs.

Timeshares have very little resale value; owners rarely get back the price they paid for them. To combat this the market has developed a points system valuing a property according to the property itself, the number of weeks purchased and the time of the year purchased. Points can be used to swap one property for another owned by the same company. Some large organisations allow points to be spent on travel products other than accommodation.

LEASEBACK

While timeshare has its critics, leaseback, a system found in large up-market developments, does not. It is a clever scheme in which it is possible to buy a property at a substantial discount of around 40 per cent in return for agreeing to occupy it for only a few weeks each year and to lease it back to the developer for the rest of the time to be let to holiday tenants. The developer also retains responsibility for maintenance and managing the property. This arrangement lasts for a period of ten years after which the owner gains full, unrestricted ownership. The owner, not the developer, is registered in the *escritura* at the full price, not the discount price.

For someone aged around 50 wanting a holiday home and ten years later a permanent retirement residence, this is a good option. It is much better value than timeshare and outright occupation.

CO-OWNERSHIP

Co-ownership is an arrangement whereby ownership of a whole property is shared between several people, who divide up the time they use it each year at fixed times (rather like a timeshare). The names of all individuals involved are entered in the *escritura* as joint owners. These schemes are offered by developers who stay in charge of ongoing property management for a fee.

Other co-ownership arrangements can be set up privately by groups of people who, by banding together, can afford to take on a much larger property than they could ever pay for on their own. The financial share of ownership need not be equal. If any co owner wishes to sell, the others normally have right of first refusal. The property can be owned by a company in the form of shares.

FURTHER READING AND INFORMATION

Harry King, *Buy to Let in Spain*. Oxford: How to Books. The Spanish way of doing it!

Liz Hodgkinson, *The Complete Guide to Letting Property*. London: Kogan Page. The English way!

Robert Irwin, *Buy, Rent and Sell*. Maidenhead: McGraw Hill. How they do it in the USA.

Timeshare: www.rci.co.uk and www.keyworldinvest.com

12

Public Services, Customs Control and Consumer Protection

INTRODUCTION

Foreign residents and visitors to Spain find that Embassies and Consulates provide an important link to their homeland. They represent the interests of their subjects and provide assistance in many different ways.

For Spaniards and foreign residents too, a local focal point is the *ayuntamiento* (town hall) invariably situated in the main square of each village, town or city and easily spotted by national flags flying outside.

Schools have, in the main, good academic reputations with multi-language opportunities. The state health service is excellent with standards improving all the time.

Goods move freely within the EU with Andorra, Gibraltar and Morocco providing additional opportunities for duty-free shopping.

The consumer is well protected as all businesses are required by law to keep a complaints book or complaints forms (*libros/hojas de reclamaciones*) which must be produced on demand. And there is the *Oficina Municipal de Informacion al Consumidor* (*OMIC*), defending a customer from unscrupulous suppliers.

BRITISH EMBASSY AND CONSULATE

The British Embassy has overall responsibility for representing and promoting the UK in Spain. The consular section provides services for British citizens in Spain and visas for those who require them to travel to the UK. The British Consulate General in Madrid is the issuing authority for all UK passports and visas in Spain. Other British Consulates in Spain can issue emergency passports, valid only for a one-way journey to the UK. The Madrid Consulate registers the births and deaths of British citizens resident in or visiting Spain.

Application forms for passports and visas are available by post or to personal callers, or can be downloaded direct from their website on www.ukinspain.com. The site also offers information on subjects ranging from timeshares to travel information.

The Consulate can:

- Issue emergency passports (see Chapter 2).

- Contact friends and relatives to ask them to help with money and tickets.

- Supply information on a number of topics.

- In an emergency, cash a sterling cheque up to £100 if supported by a valid banker's card or as a last resort give a loan to get someone back to the UK.

- Help with local lawyers, interpreters and doctors in the case of death.

The Consulate cannot:

- Intervene in court cases or get someone out of prison.

- Give legal advice, start court proceedings or investigate a crime.

- Pay travel costs, hotel, legal, medical or any other bills.

- Find a person somewhere to live, a job or a work permit.

- Formally help a person with dual nationality where the second nationality is Spanish.

THE TOWN HALL

To the ordinary Spaniard politics start and stop at the *ayuntamiento* (town hall). Situated in the Plaza Mayor of each village, town or city the building is bedecked with a national flag together with flags of the *Comunidad* and the Province signifying its importance as a focus in everyday life. The town hall is the home of the *Municipio*, a council headed by a mayor (*alcalde*) and a number of councillors (*concejales*) all of whom are elected. The *ayuntamiento* is responsible for keeping the streets clean, collecting garbage, street lighting, water supply and sewerage, roads, cemeteries, schools, planning, parks, libraries, markets, social services, fire prevention and public sports facilities. It is where local taxes are paid, licences are issued, applications for building permits are lodged, the right to vote is granted and births, marriages and deaths are recorded.

Signing on the *Padron*

A foreigner's first encounter with the *ayuntamiento* will probably be to register as a new resident of the town and consequently be allowed to stand and vote at elections.

- Visit the town hall with a passport and evidence of residing in the town (*copia simple* or *escritura* or *residencia*)

- Complete some details. Provided more than six months each year is spent residing in the municipality and the individual is not registered in another municipality at the same time, you will now be on the census of inhabitants residing in the area administered by that *ayuntamiento*.

- An *Empadronamiento Certificate* (census registration certificate) is issued.

Not everyone wishes to vote. Who are the candidates? What do they stand for? An

EU citizen signing on the *padron* is entitled to vote in local elections and can be elected to office. They can also vote for their local European parliamentary representative or again stand for office. One per cent of councillors in coastal regions are foreigners. The only additional qualification is to speak Spanish.

One method of communicating with the *ayuntamiento* is to present a request or complaint in writing which will be stamped *recibido* (received) on presentation and must be acted upon in a reasonable period of time.

The greater number of people registered on the *padron*, the greater funds received from regional government.

Collecting taxes

One role of the town hall is to collect local taxes. This operational role detracts from its political and management role. Consequently it has been subcontracted in some provinces to a third party. *Gestion Tributaria Diputacion de Alicante*, known as *SUMA*, undertakes this for the province of Alicante. *SUMA* manages local taxes authorised by town halls, provincial councils and other public organisations from most of the 140 municipalities that form Alicante province. They are responsible for collecting *IBI* (*Impuesto Sobre Bienes Inmuebles* – a local tax based on property value), *IVTM* (motor vehicle tax), a tax for rubbish collection and other local taxes.

IBI is a local tax, rather like rates/poll tax/council tax in the UK but at a fraction of the cost. The services offered by a municipality are considerably less than in the UK. Home owners may have to take their rubbish to a central collection point. Street cleaners are rarely evident. Social services exist, but only to a limited degree. An *IBI* bill for a town house may only be 100€ per year reflecting a level of service, a degree of central funding... and more importantly an artificially low level of property valuation. However this has to be balanced against Community charges for a private development which can be as high as 1,500€ per annum reflecting shared costs for roads, pools, gardens and lifts.

Assessment of *IBI* is based on the fiscal value (*valor catastral*) of a property. The *IBI* tax rate is 0.3 per cent for agricultural properties (*rusticas*) and 0.5 per cent for urban properties (*urbana*). However, provincial capitals, towns with over 5,000 inhabitants and towns providing special services can increase the rate to up to 1.7 per cent. To calculate an *IBI* bill multiply the fiscal value by the tax rate. A property with a fiscal value of 25,000€ in a village with a tax rate of 0.5 per cent will have an *IBI* bill of 125€ per year.

SUMA is an enlightened organisation pushing Spain's administration systems well into the twenty-first century by bringing tax management close to the citizen through a computer based decentralisation process. They are able to efficiently and immediately inform a citizen about their local taxes, thus altering the traditional face of Spanish officialdom. *SUMA* acts all year round. Nevertheless there are two special periods for voluntary collection. The first period is from March to May. The second period runs from August to October. Payment of local taxes after these periods attracts a surcharge.

SCHOOLS

The Spanish educational system

Schooling is compulsory between 6 and 16 years of age. Below the age of 6 years schooling is optional and dependent on availability in the immediate area. It is common to send children to school from about the age of 3 years but starting infant school at this age is not compulsory. Although the academic year runs from September until June, children start compulsory schooling in the September of the calendar year in which they are 6 years old. In order to progress from one cycle of education to the next, students in Spanish state schools have to meet teaching and learning objectives. Compulsory schooling could last longer than in the UK where students progress from one year to the next automatically.

A Certificate of Secondary Education is awarded at the end of compulsory secondary education to students who achieve the required grades. They can leave the education system or can apply for either academic or technical *Bachillerato* vocational training. Students with appropriate qualifications and wishing to progress to a university in Spain usually take an entrance exam. The Certificate of Secondary Education is not inferior to a number of GCSEs and the *Bachillerato* is not inferior to A levels. Therefore students obtaining the appropriate grades required for entrance into universities in the UK are not precluded because they have Spanish qualifications.

Parents must pay for books, materials and any extra-curricular activities. Low income families may be able to get a grant for these items. School uniform is not always a prerequisite.

Spanish schools

Spanish schools can be state or privately owned. Fees are payable in some private schools but not all. Some private schools subsidised by the Spanish government are, if you like, 'grant maintained' and therefore tuition is provided free.

The language of instruction is Spanish or a combination of Spanish and a regional language. Teachers employed in the state sector do not necessarily speak English and in any event lessons are not taught in English. If English is taught as a foreign language, which is mostly the case, there is an English teacher at the school whose main job is to teach English as a foreign language.

The school year runs from about mid-September until about the end of June, but dates vary according to age group and region. There are no half-terms as such but there are other holidays besides Easter and Christmas which vary according to where one lives.

To apply for a place at a Spanish state school which is publicly funded you need the parents' passports, the child's full birth certificate, marriage papers and documentary evidence of domicile in Spain. For older children, age 14 upwards, it may be necessary to have results of their studies in the UK officially validated.

International schools

There are a growing number of international schools in Spain that follow a British curriculum. Fees for day students are usually cheaper than school fees in the UK but demand for places can be high. Some English speaking private international schools follow the American curriculum, rather than the British one. Whichever style is chosen, most international schools are required to teach a small part of the Spanish curriculum in addition to the international one.

Bilingual schools

There are few private schools in Spain with bilingual programmes. These are different from most international schools because children will be taught in more than one language. Many bilingual schools are private schools in that they do not receive any funding from the Spanish government but some grant maintained private schools offer a bilingual education too.

Statistics

Education statistics make interesting reading. Thirty per cent of Spanish schoolchildren are currently being educated in private schools, most of which are co-educational day schools. Ninety per cent of all children between the age of 4 and 5 attend nursery school and over 55 per cent of students remain at school until their 18th birthday. Of these, a further 25 per cent go on to vocational training and 30 per cent to university.

Foreign children

As with any state system, Spanish schooling is not without criticism, some complaining it is weighed down with traditional and unimaginative teaching methods, poorly paid and poorly motivated teachers. But this view is not universal. One UK mother of 5 children has nothing but praise for the Spanish school system. She was delighted that her children were doing so well at school and, more importantly, were happy, well adjusted kids.

The younger a child when entering the Spanish school system, the easier they cope. The language is assimilated quickly and although the first month can be traumatic, it isn't long before young children are speaking Spanish well. It is also the case that the older child has greater problems. Teenagers find it much more difficult learning the language, integrating socially and dealing with a demanding school curriculum. The result is an unhappy child at a difficult time in life and poor school results.

It is understandable that so many older foreign children coming to live in Spain are sent to private, English run schools. Here they can continue in the education system they know and at the same time learn Spanish. Many expatriates with younger children choose to start their child's education in Spanish nursery and primary schools and then switch their secondary education to a private school.

Most foreign children cope well with being educated in Spain be it private or state education. Living in a foreign land is an adventure which offers both change and challenge and most rise to the occasion. In no time at all their thinking becomes international, allowing their behaviour to become the same in later life. Spanish children are aware that the EU is made up of many different nationalities as most attend schools with pupils from different countries.

HEALTH SYSTEM

The Spanish are healthy people. Their diet of fish, fresh fruit and vegetables, olive oil instead of unsaturated fats, plus a glass of red wine per day contributes to this. For sufferers of rheumatism, arthritis and bronchitis, Spain's climate is therapeutic. A relaxed lifestyle can have a positive effect on mental health since it is a well-known fact that people who live in sunnier climates are generally happier than those who live in cold, wet climates.

Spain has no special health risks apart from over indulgence. The tap water is in the main drinkable, although during periods of shortage the quality may suffer and people revert to a bottled variety. Drink the red wine too, which is plentiful, cheap and beneficial when consumed in moderation.

Complaints associated with smoking-related ailments are high. Smoking is the leading cause of death among adults, with cheap cigarettes causing 55,000 deaths per year, no doubt because Spain has the second highest number of smokers in the EU.

Health care facilities are good. Medical staff are highly trained and hospitals equipped with the latest technology. The public and private systems live happily together. The Red Cross also makes an important contribution.

Visitors

EU residents visiting Spain can take advantage of health care agreements providing their home country has a reciprocal agreement with Spain. The UK does. EU residents should apply for a certificate of entitlement to treatment, known as form E111, from their local post office three weeks before planning to travel. The E111 is valid for three months only and must be stamped prior to departure. If the E111 is used for valid emergency or urgent medical treatment, present the form plus a photocopy to the medical practitioner or hospital providing the treatment. If payment is required obtain a receipt, and apply for reimbursement back home.

A person under retirement age who has paid regular social security contributions in another EU country for two full years prior to coming to Spain is entitled to public health cover for a period of six months by remitting costs of treatment to their former social security system. For ex-UK residents this benefit is approved in advance by the Social Security office in Newcastle.

New permanent residents

Temporary health cover administered through form E111 is not an acceptable solution for Spain's new permanent residents. It is of course possible to take out medical insurance, which is one way of dealing with this issue. Emergencies, visits to the doctor and hospital are normally covered by such a policy but medicines and dental treatment are not.

Public health benefits, under the Spanish state health scheme called *INSALUD* (*Instituto Nacional de la Salud*), include general and specialist medical care, hospitalisation, laboratory services, medicines, maternity and some dental care. Anyone who pays regular social security contributions to *INSALUD* by virtue of their employment is entitled, for themselves and family, to free medical treatment.

Free entry into the scheme is allowed for:

- EU residents holding a *residencia* who are in receipt of a state pension and are over 60 (woman) or 65 (man).

- A dependant of someone (wife or husband) can also enter the scheme provided they are both residents of Spain. For example a man not yet 65, who is married to a wife who is 60, is regarded as a dependant and both are entitled to enter the scheme.

- EU nationals, resident in Spain, who are disabled or receive invalidity benefit.

- EU nationals of retirement age, but not in receipt of a pension, may be entitled to health benefits.

Here is the procedure to obtain a *Tarjeta de Sanitaria* (health card):

- Obtain form E121 from the Social Security Office back home.

- Assemble a *residencia* (or proof of application), a passport and a copy, and *NIE*.

- Go to the appropriate social security office to complete some paperwork.

- Follow directions to a nominated medical centre which will allocate a doctor.

What to do in an emergency

Emergency medical services in most EU countries, including Spain, are good. In a life-threatening emergency call for an ambulance and mention the nature of the emergency. Telephone numbers, which can vary from province to province, are in the phone book, near the start, under the heading *Servicos de Urgencia*. Ambulances come under the umbrella of social security ambulances, Red Cross ambulances or 24-hour private medical centre ambulances. They are equipped with emergency equipment and staff trained to provide first-aid. The ambulance service is usually free.

Taxis must, by law, transport medical emergencies to hospital when requested to do so. A private car can claim priority when transporting a medical emergency by switching on its hazard warning lights and waving a piece of white material from the window.

In an emergency go to the hospital casualty department, or a 24-hour public health clinic. It may be important to check which local hospitals are equipped to deal with the situation. In an emergency a hospital must treat you, regardless of your ability to pay.

Doctors

Finding a doctor who speaks English can be a problem. In the public sector the doctors are Spanish and are unlikely to speak English. In the private sector, particularly in cities and resort areas, there are many English-speaking German and Scandinavian doctors. Private sector doctors advertise their services in the expatriate press.

Private health insurance allows an individual to choose a doctor from a list provided. Within the public sector the choice is nil – the patient is allocated a doctor. Within the private sector specialists do not require patients to have a doctor's referral although this is necessary in the public sector.

Chemists

A chemist (*farmacia*) is recognised by the sign of a green cross. The address of the nearest 24-hour chemist and a list of duty chemists are posted outside and also published in local newspapers. A pharmacist in Spain must own and run their own business. Chains of chemist shops are illegal.

Private prescriptions cost 100 per cent of the cost of medicines. Prescriptions under the public health scheme cost 40 per cent, or nothing at all for a pensioner or disabled person. General medication, such as aspirin or cough medicine which can be purchased in supermarkets in some countries, can only be purchased from a *farmacia* in Spain. Chemists are highly trained and provide free medical advice for minor ailments. They are able to sell remedies without recourse to a doctor and can supply a wide range of medicines without prescription.

Chemists sell prescription drugs, non-prescription medicines, cosmetics, diet foods and toiletries. A *drogueria* sells non-medical items such as toiletries, cosmetics and household cleaning items, but not medicines. A *herboristeria* sells health foods, diet foods and herbal remedies.

Hospitals

Hospitales de la seguridad social (public hospitals) and *hospitals privados* (private hospitals) are the core of the health system together with other establishments such as nursing homes, emergency clinics and analyses laboratories. Admittance or referral to a hospital or clinic for treatment is by a doctor or a specialist. It is possible to leave hospital at any time by signing a release form.

For private patients it is essential to provide evidence of health insurance or the ability to pay. If a private insurance company does not have an arrangement with a hospital to pay direct, then the bill has to be paid by the individual and the cost reclaimed.

Spanish families are accustomed to looking after their relatives while in hospital and even after they return home. Patients are still expected to convalesce at home, not in a hospital, and they are often discharged earlier than would be the case in many other countries.

Most foreigners are very satisfied with treatment in Spanish hospitals. The difference in treatment varies little between the best public and private hospitals. It stands comparison with the best the UK can offer.

Dentists

There are many private English-speaking dentists. They are permitted to advertise their services and do so freely. Dentists expect to be paid immediately after treatment is completed.

Opticians

Although the optical business is highly competitive (simply count the number of shops in a main street) and prices for spectacles are not controlled, it is surprising to find glasses are more expensive in Spain than in other European countries. An ophthalmologist in Spain is the same as anywhere else – a specialist doctor trained in diagnosing and treating disorders of the eye, performing sight tests, and prescribing spectacles and contact lenses.

CUSTOMS CONTROL

The relatively free movement of people and goods within the EU means customs officials are rarely seen. Border posts are now unmanned boundaries as vehicles move freely between France, Portugal and Spain. Regular air travellers between the UK and Spain may have their passports checked when leaving and entering the UK but rarely when entering Spain. Since 1993 there have been no cross-border shopping restrictions within the EU for goods purchased duty and tax paid, providing all goods are for personal consumption or use and not for resale. Although there are no restrictions, there are levels for items such as spirits, wine, beer and tobacco products, above which goods may be classified as commercial quantities. Duty free shopping within the EU ended in 1999, although it is still available when travelling outside the EU.

Things are different however, very different, when entering Spain from Andorra, Gibraltar and Morocco. These countries open up an opportunity for duty-free shopping, or in the case of Morocco shopping outside the EU. While Gibraltar is convenient for ex-pats living on the Costa del Sol, it is Andorra which is Europe's biggest duty-free shop with considerable savings being made on alcohol, tobacco, food, watches, cameras, electrical goods, perfume, luxury goods and petrol[1].

For each journey to a non-EU country such as Morocco, travellers aged 17 or over are entitled to import the following goods purchased duty-free. As duty-free allowances apply both to the outward and return journey, the combined total of double the limit can be imported back home:

- one litre of spirits (over 22° proof) or two litres of fortified wine, sparkling wine or other liqueurs (under 22° proof);

- two litres of still table wine;

- 200 cigarettes or 100 cigarillos or 50 cigars or 250g of tobacco;

---

1 People do not visit Morocco, Gibraltar or Andorra solely for shopping. Morocco has an exotic taste of Africa, Gibraltar a taste of the old country and Andorra … what can be said about a small town where terrifying mountains encroach on pavements and where nobody, but nobody, ever smiles, where shops offer luxury goods at a fraction of a discount on any normal shopping centre in Europe, where the barman of a fancy café looks with inquiring eyes and never says a word of welcome, where…? Perhaps Andorra is best seen covered in snow.

- 50cc of perfume;

- 250cc of toilet water;

- other goods including gifts and souvenirs to the value of 175€ such as rugs, leather goods and spices.

To and from Andorra the duty free limits are:

- 1.5 litres of alcohol over 22° proof or 3 litres of alcohol under 22° proof;

- 5 litres of still table wine;

- 300 cigarettes or 150 cigarillos or 75 cigars or 400g of pipe tobacco;

- 75g of perfume and 375ml of toilet water;

- up to 175€ worth of agricultural goods, although there are limits for some products such as milk (6 litres), butter (1kg), cheese (4kg), sugar (5kg), coffee (1kg) and tea (200g);

- up to 525€ worth of manufactured goods such as electrical and luxury items.

Duty free allowances for Gibraltar are:

- 200 cigarettes;

- one bottle of spirits;

- 200 litres of petrol;

- any other purchases to the value of 175€ such as goods from English chain stores.

A resident outside the EU can reclaim Value Added Tax (*IVA*) on single purchases over 100€ made in Spain. Large items can be sent directly abroad and *IVA* will not be added. At airports it can also be reclaimed at a special Europe Tax Free Shopping refund area. For smaller purchases an export sales invoice is provided by retailers which is registered by a customs officer upon leaving Spain, with an *IVA* refund posted or credited to a card.

CONSUMER PROTECTION

Shopping

All products sold must be suitable for the use for which they are intended. If found at fault one is entitled to an exchange or a full refund irrespective of whether goods were purchased at full or discounted price. Always keep a receipt (*recibo*) as a complaint will not be entertained without one. Make a complaint within 14 days or it can be dismissed. In addition, normal consumer protection laws exist for products and services where complaints should be made direct to a supplier or manufacturer.

Oficina Municipal de Informacion al Consumidor

The Ministry of Health and Consumer Affairs (*Ministerio de Sanidad y Consumo*) has local offices called *Oficina Municipal de Informacion al Consumidor* or *OMIC*. *OMIC* offices are established in liaison with town halls. *OMIC* is not limited to basic consumer problems such as defective goods or incorrect prices. They can deal with broader issues relating to timeshare and property rentals. *OMIC* offices are helpful and make an effort to see action is taken. A serious complaint may be referred to the *OMIC* regional office in a regional capital. A business can be fined a substantial amount if a complaint is upheld.

Asociaciones de Amas de Casa

Housewife associations have both a watchdog and an educational role. These organisations generally require membership in order to benefit from their services. The main consumer organisation in Spain is the *Organizacion de Consumidores y Usuarios* (www.ocu.org). *OCU* runs a programme to inform tourists of their rights and publishes a magazine called *Compra Maestra*.

Serious complaints

A serious complaint concerning weights and measures can be directed to the *Jefatura Provincial de Comercio Interior* (Provincial Department of Internal Commerce).

This office is responsible for correct weights, and checking that prices are within limits on controlled items and products are up to standard.

Exhausted all administrative channels? The ombudsman or Defender of the People is the last resort when justice has not been done. If going to the *OMIC* fails to bring the desired result, or if unjustly treated by any government agency, then try the *Defensor del Pueblo*, the regional ombudsman.

Other procedures

There are special complaints procedures for many organisations including utility companies, the post office, public transport companies, insurance companies and the public health service. Professional associations covering *abogados*, doctors and such like have their own complaint procedures. The best known is banking, for every Spanish bank has its own central *Defensor del Cliente* (Defender of the Customer), who will hear a complaint when no satisfaction has been obtained from a branch office.

Hoja de Reclamacion

All businesses are required by law to keep a complaints book or complaints forms (*libros/hojas de reclamaciones*), which must be produced on demand. Requesting a complaints form often results in a speedy and satisfactory outcome to a dispute as copies of all complaints must be forwarded to the authorities within 48 hours. The *hoja de reclamacion* comes in three copies. The business keeps one copy and the customer takes the other two, one to keep and the other to present at the local *OMIC* office if necessary. A business must respond to a client's complaint within ten days. If it does not the consumer can take their case to the *OMIC* and the business can face a fine.

FURTHER INFORMATION

British Embassy and Consulate	www.ukinspain.com
Ayuntamiento	www.ayuntamiento de … [name of town]
Schools	Minesterio de Educacion y Ciencia. Tel: 917 018 000 or www.mec.es

British Council	Tel: 913 373 500 or www.britishcouncil.es
Health system	UK Department of Health and Social Security. Tel: 0191 218 7777 or www.dwp.gov.uk Spain. Tel: INSULAD 900 166 563 or www.seg-social.es
Customs control	www.hmrc.gov.uk

13
Working in Spain

INTRODUCTION

Working conditions are controlled by the 1984 Workers' Statute and other related agreements such as collective terms, an employee's individual employment contract and an employer's in-house rules. Employees are protected by this statute prohibiting discrimination on the grounds of sex, marital status, age, race, social status, religious belief, political opinion and trade union membership. Discrimination is also illegal on grounds of mental or physical disability, providing a disabled person is able to perform the work required.

There has traditionally been an assumed link between an employment contract and a job for life. This situation has changed dramatically in recent years, during which Spain's labour problems have been exacerbated by the unions' uncompromising defence of rigid employment terms. Spain has the most rigid labour market in Europe and is a major headache to employers. In spite of an agreement reached between the employers and unions in 1997, where unions reduced their entitlement to redundancy payments in return for permanent contracts, employers still hire 90 per cent of new employees on a temporary contract.

INEM

Spanish job centres are called the *INEM* (*Instituto Nacional de Empleo*). *INEM* operates 700 offices throughout Spain advertising both local and national positions. Vacancies in the local area are advertised on a bulletin board, together with some national positions requiring experience, training or qualifications. *INEM* offices provide a comprehensive career resource library including Spanish company listings, trade publications and a wide range of reference books. In addition to offering a job placement service, *INEM* also provides assistance to those wishing to start a business or be self-employed.

Speaking the language

The most important requirement for anyone seeking employment or running a business is the ability to speak good Spanish. Regional languages and dialects cause problems for foreigners and Spaniards alike but if seeking to earn money, learning the language *Castellano*, or a regional variation, is the only option. Lack of a second language restricts business opportunities to within the English speaking community. While English may be the language of international business, dealing with Spanish people, or fitting into a multilingual work environment requires an ability to converse in Spanish. Working in Spain for a multinational company, a UK company, or for one whose name is recognisable worldwide can offer security. However teams of Spanish nationals run Spanish branches of multinational companies and most of the work is conducted in their language. You need to fit in.

WORK PERMIT

For European Union nationals

An EU national does not require a permit to enter Spain for work. You can enter Spain as a tourist, register with the Spanish national employment office *INEM* and then have 90 days to find employment. It is possible to obtain an extension after that date, or leave Spain and re-enter for a further 90 days. Once a job is secured an employment contract is necessary to apply for a *residencia*. In actual fact it is a *trajeta comunitaria* which is a combined work permit and *residencia*. It also comes with an *NIE*.

Surprisingly this is done by an employer. For people setting up a business simply start by obtaining a *residencia* and follow guidelines later in this chapter.

For non-EU nationals

A non-EU foreigner who wishes to work in Spain must obtain a visa before moving to Spain. Work permits can be obtained from the Foreigners' Office (*Oficinas de Extranjeros*) or the provincial office of the Ministry of Labour (*Delegacion Provincial del Ministerio de Trabajo*), if the foreign applicant is on Spanish territory. The provincial labour offices (*Direciones Provinciales de Trabajo, Seguridad Social y Asuntos Sociales*) will decide whether a work permit will be issued. If the foreign applicant is not in Spain the work permit is obtained from the Consular office of the applicant's home country at the same time as obtaining a visa. Documents required for an application for a work permit are:

For an employee:

- copy of valid passport;

- certificate of criminal records issued by the authorities of the foreigner's home country;

- official medical certificate;

- three passport-size photographs;

- fiscal registration number (*NIE*) and the social security registration number of the employer;

- a formal offer of employment;

- full description of the job and the company activity.

For the self-employed:

- copy of valid passport;

- certificate of criminal records issued by the authorities of the foreigner's home country;

- official medical certificate;

- three passport-size photographs;

- full description of the job and the company activity;

- proof of professional qualifications to perform the activity in Spain;

- appropriate business licences, fiscal registration number (*NIE*) and social security registration number.

Types of work permit

Where the foreigner is an employee

- **Type A work permit**: for seasonal or time limited work. This may entail a specific contract or a specific geographic area. Its maximum duration is nine months.

- **Type B initial work permit**: enables the foreigner to work in a specific profession, activity and geographic area for a maximum period of one year.

- **Type B renewed work permit**: issued to Type B holders once that has expired. It is an entitlement to carry on various professions or activities for a maximum period of two years.

- **Type C work permit**: issued to Type B renewed work permit holders once that has expired. This entitles the foreign worker to perform any professional activity throughout Spain.

Where the foreigner is self-employed

- **Type D initial work permit**: to carry on a specific activity for a maximum of one year. Spanish authorities can limit this to a specific geographic area.

- **Type D renewed work permit**: issued to those Type D initial holders once it has expired. It entitles the holder to perform various professional activities for a maximum period of two years. Spanish labour authorities could limit this to a specific geographic area and/or a specific activity.

- **Type E work permit**: issued to those holding the Type D renewed work permit once it has expired. This entitles the foreign worker to perform any professional activity throughout the Spanish Territory for a maximum period of three years.

Where the foreigner is an employee or self-employed

- **Type F work permit**: to perform professional activities within Spanish borders provided they return daily to the foreign country of residence e.g. Gibraltar. This is issued for a maximum period of five years, after that it may be renewed.

- **Permanent work permit**: enables foreign workers to perform any professional activity where they have the qualification required. The Type C or E work permit holders may obtain this work permit once theirs has expired. It is mandatory to renew this work permit every five years.

- **Extraordinary work permit**: issued to non-EU foreign citizens who have helped the Spanish economic and cultural progress. It enables a foreign worker to perform any professional activity throughout Spain if they have the qualification required. This must be renewed every five years.

CASUAL AND SEASONAL, PART-TIME OR FULL-TIME AND PROFESSIONAL WORK

Casual and seasonal work

This type of work is ideal for anyone who has not firmed up a long-term life plan, or who seeks a few euros while enjoying life in the sun. It is not too easy to come by, usually involves lots of asking around, and may need a personal recommendation. Casual work is more likely to be found in tourist regions where there is a seasonal demand for labour. It is likely to be paid in cash by an employer not wishing to incur any social security costs. When business demand is low – no work, but the employer will be happy to welcome the employee back when tourists return.

It can be easy to get carried away by the seemingly casual lifestyle, a laid-back approach and amicable sales methods in tourist areas, but remember it is profit and customer service that counts. Don't assume that working for an English speaking

Northern European gives added security. Spain is full of ex-pats who for one reason or another have decided to make a living through running a bar or a shop where the business is often very fragile or seasonal.

Examples of casual or seasonal work are:

- villa servicing and cleaning;

- promotional work;

- nursing and auxiliary nursing in hospitals, clinics and nursing homes;

- bar, restaurant and hotel work;

- holiday rep with a major tourist company. This is one of the best sources of seasonal work for foreigners. Competition for jobs is fierce and some Spanish fluency is usually necessary. Most companies have an age requirement.

Part-time and full-time work

For someone staying long-term, some help may be found from the few, relatively new, employment agencies, but asking around is also essential. Without a command of the language employment is again restricted to holiday regions. Procedures for finding a job are exactly the same as back home. Newspaper adverts, employment agencies, direct contact with companies, word of mouth and personal contact are all necessary. A good CV in English and Spanish, to sell your skills, is helpful. Working full- or part-time involves a different working day, correct business etiquette, payment of social security and income tax. Examples are:

- office work;

- English type supermarkets;

- journalism and advertising with local English newspapers and magazines;

- teaching English;

- working in an estate agent's office.

People who are fluent in Spanish and English can find work in the major cities as translators where the task involves business correspondence, or assisting Northern Europeans with some Spanish paperwork, or even at police stations on busy market days where petty theft is common and an interpreter necessary.

British entertainers often report a lack of motivation and an authoritarian style while working for Spanish employers. Other people too question the less than democratic skills and employment practices of Spanish companies. 'Unquestionably sharp' is a phrase often used to describe abuse of employment contracts in a situation where an unsuspecting foreigner does not fully understand employment law.

Professional qualifications

Professionals whose training consisted of at least three years' degree level education plus job-based training require their qualifications to be recognised subject to any professional codes and limitations in force. For example doctors must have their qualifications accepted by the medical college of the province where they intend to practice. They must also show that they are in good standing with the professional authorities in their country of origin.

All EU member states issue occupation information sheets containing a common job description with a table of qualifications. These cover a large number of trades and are intended to help someone with the relevant qualifications look for employment in another EU country. In order to have their qualifications recognised in Spain *homologiacion* is necessary (see Chapter 3). The starting point for information regarding the official validation of qualifications and the addresses of Spanish professional bodies is obtainable from the education department of Spanish consulates.

Teaching

Staying long-term in Spain? Then the chances of finding teaching work are considerably better than for any other profession although this obviously depends on qualifications and experience. Teaching English is big business. Spanish nationals wish to have a second language. For commercial reasons it has to be English. There is a constant demand for teachers. People with a Teaching English as a Foreign Language qualification or English as a Second Language certificate can find a job quite easily. Where demand outstrips supply in the big cities a graduate native English speaker can get a job without other qualifications. Some of the opportunities are:

- Private language schools in Spain offer English classes for both adults and children.

- English teachers and teachers employed in language schools supplement their income by giving private lessons.

- The British Council in Madrid recruits English language teachers and supervisory staff for two-year placements in its language centres in Barcelona, Bilbao, Granada, Las Palmas, Madrid, Oviedo, Palma de Mallorca, Segovia, Seville and Valencia.

- Being a language assistant enables students from Britain and more than 30 other countries to spend a year working in a school or college in Spain assisting language teachers.

CONTRACT OF EMPLOYMENT

Spanish employees now have an affluent lifestyle compared to their parents in the Years of Hunger. They enjoy high salaries (particularly executives and senior managers) and good working conditions. Women have professional and wage equality with men, although they still fill most low-paid jobs. Employment security has been eroded in recent years with an increasing number of workers employed on short-term rather than indefinite employment contracts, giving some flexibility in the labour market. Some low-paid people hold down two jobs, rather like their civil service forefathers in the 1960s.

Although employment conditions vary throughout Europe, the main areas for comparison are salary level, fringe benefits and job security. Spanish employees are near the bottom of the European earnings league, but good fringe benefits, lots of holidays, job security and strong protection under dismissal legislation are undoubted plus factors.

Spain has lost more production days due to strikes in the last 15 years than any country in the EU. Contrary to the UK, the government can enforce an imposed settlement if a strike impairs public services or disrupts important sectors of the economy. Employees are also guaranteed the right to strike under law and cannot be dismissed for striking.

The contract

Employees in Spain, like other parts of Europe, have an employment contract (*contrato de trabajo*) stating details such as job title, salary, working hours, fringe benefits and the terms of employment. There are three types of employment contract:

- An indefinite term contract.

- A short-term temporary contract for a specific duration and reason, for example, a contract for a specific project or service, or for six months to deal with peak demand, or to substitute for another employee who is entitled to return to work.

- A verbal or written contract for casual or seasonal work, which gives few legal rights.

All employment contracts are subject to Spanish labour law and references may be made to other regulations such as collective agreements. Anything in contracts contrary to the statutory provisions and unfavourable to an employee is deemed to be null and void. If there is no written contract, the law assumes that the verbal agreement is for one year. At the end of this year, or at any other time, the employer can dismiss the worker, giving at least seven days' notice and paying seven days' salary for each full year worked.

Salary

A salary is stated in the employment contract together with any salary reviews, planned increases and cost of living reviews. Salaries can be paid weekly, fortnightly or monthly, by cash or into a bank account. A pay slip itemising salary and deductions is issued. Spain has a minimum wage. At around 3€ per hour it is a meaningless figure in the labour market, useful only to trades unions seeking a marker for annual wage increases.

Extra months' salary and bonuses

Employers in Spain pay their employees two extra months' salary – one paid in July before the annual summer holiday and the other in December – which is intended to ensure that employees have extra money for their summer and Christmas holidays. Taking statutory, local fiesta days and annual holidays into account Spanish employees get 14 months' salary for ten months' work.

Working hours

The standard working week in Spain is 40 hours. The average with overtime is around 42 hours. Working hours vary depending on the profession (manual/office/government/service) and time of year (summer/winter). The standard working day is from 9.30am to 13.30pm and from 16.30pm until 20.30pm; although from June to September it may be continuous from 7.00am to 15.00pm with a short break for lunch. In line with their European counterparts many companies now operate from 8.30am or 9.00am to 17.30pm or 18.00pm. There are no scheduled coffee breaks but it's common for office workers in a town or city to pop out for breakfast, or a cup of coffee, twice a day during business hours.

Overtime

Overtime is not compulsory and cannot exceed 80 hours a year. It must be paid at a premium not less than 40 per cent of the normal hourly rate and 100 per cent for Sunday and statutory holidays. Employees are not obliged to work on Sundays unless a collective agreement states otherwise, although when an employee agrees to work on a Sunday, normal overtime rates are applicable. Overtime may be compensated for by time off rather than extra pay, providing there is a written agreement to that effect.

Social security

All employers and their employees, including foreign, temporary and permanent employees, must contribute to the Spanish social security system (*seguridad social*).

Social security for employees covers health care (including sickness and maternity leave), injuries at work, unemployment insurance, retirement benefit, invalidity and death benefit. Pension benefits starts only after 15 years' contributions. Unemployment benefit starts if you have worked for 360 days during the last six years and registered with the *INEM* within 15 days of unemployment.

There are special social security programmes for agricultural workers, seamen, self-employed workers, civil servants and military personnel, coal miners and students. For everybody else there is a general social security programme where people are classified under a number of professional categories in order to determine their social security contribution. Payment is based on a *nomina*, the official salary for a classification of work, with the employee's contribution deducted at source by the employer. Social security contributions by the employee are around five per cent and by the employer 23 per cent. The total contribution is around 28 per cent – an extraordinarily large figure on a minimum base salary of 760€ per month.

Spain has treaty agreements with other countries ensuring someone who has worked in two or more countries does not retire with a pension deficit. These agreements ensure that the total number of years paid into social security systems in the various countries are added together to enable the employee to qualify for a pension which is paid proportionally by each country.

Public holidays

The government allows 14 national and local public holidays a year. Of these, two are regional or municipal holidays celebrating dates of local importance. All public offices, banks and post offices are closed on public holidays. In addition most regions and towns have their own carnival and fiesta days.

Annual holidays

Under law a full-time employee is entitled to a minimum of 23 working days (one month) paid annual holiday. When both annual and public holidays are taken into account, Spain has the greatest number of holidays of any EU country. August is the traditional month for summer holidays, with many businesses closing down entirely.

Some businesses close for two weeks over Christmas and New Year and many restaurants in holiday areas for the month of February.

Dismissal and redundancy

In addition to reasons such as mutual agreement, death, expiration of the contractual term and retirement, an employment contract can be collectively terminated for technological and economic reasons, and individually for objective or disciplinary reasons.

An employee can be made redundant on technological and economic grounds only in relation to the collective restructuring of a company's workforce. Technological and economic causes are legally defined terms, when the employer may decide dismissal unilaterally. Termination of employment due to redundancy attracts generous payment: eight days' pay for each year worked under temporary contracts, and 33 days' pay per year for indefinite term contracts. If a company goes bankrupt employees are entitled to 20 days' pay for each year of service.

Objective reasons for dismissal include employee ineptitude and an inability to adapt to technological change. Legal grounds for dismissal for disciplinary reasons include insubordination or disobedience, repeated absenteeism or lateness, physical or verbal abuse, fraud, disloyalty, poor performance, carrying on business on the employee's own account for a third party without the consent of the employer, and habitual drug or alcohol abuse.

An employee dismissed for objective or disciplinary reasons may challenge the decision in the labour courts. Equally an employee can leave and seek compensation if they feel an employer has not held to the terms of a contract. Disputes about these matters are taken to the *Magistratura de Trabajo*, the labour court, which will arbitrate and make a judgment.

THE BLACK ECONOMY

Illegal working is common in Spain and neighbouring Morocco. The black economy (*economia sumergida*), or the cash for services labour market, is a significant proportion of the country's generated wealth. What causes this situation?

- Influxes of illegal Moroccan immigrants seeking to better themselves in Spain are keen to accept low cash payments for unskilled work.

- It is illegal for non-EU nationals, such as Moroccans, to work in Spain without a work permit (the application is by the employer). Unscrupulous employers bypass this procedure and use this labour to pay low wages for long hours in poor working conditions. This occurs in industries traditionally employing casual labour, such as the building, farming and food service.

- Illegal working avoids payment of additional costs (particularly social security and *IVA* payments). This can make the difference between a fair product price and one that is too expensive, or the difference between profit and loss.

- Many casual, seasonal workers or indeed full-time workers choose to work illegally. They do not pay tax or social security contributions and while there is no entitlement to state benefits for work injury, health care, unemployment benefit or pension, this is viewed as a small penalty.

HAVING YOUR OWN BUSINESS

Spain is traditionally a country of small companies and sole traders. There are nearly two million families running businesses employing about 75 per cent of the working population. The majority of businesses established by foreigners in Spain are linked to leisure and catering industries or to property sales. Why? The answer is twofold: low entry capital cost and providing a service in one's mother tongue. People choose to be self-employed for the lifestyle and freedom it affords but small businesses in Spain often exist on a shoestring with their owners working extremely long hours, particularly those running bars or restaurants. Many foreigners start businesses in Spain with little research, little business acumen, no knowledge, no capital and no linguistic ability. It is asking for trouble.

The first step is to conduct appropriate market research to establish that there is a real need for a business in the area and secondly to check that all necessary licences for the proposed venture actually exist or can be obtained. These could include the Opening Licence and if appropriate a licence for serving food. The purchase of an existing business, to be run exactly as before, will not require a new opening licence, but if the nature of the business is changed a new one is required.

Obtaining legal advice

Before establishing a business it is important to talk to a number of people to obtain legal advice and to take advantage of any tax benefits or grants. This advice is usually obtained from a lawyer (*abogado*) or an accountant (*asesor fiscal*) but there are other sources too.

An excellent source of information is the commercial section of the British Embassy in Spain, known as UK Trade and Investment. They will be happy to help individual business people. This help will usually consist of providing information and contacts and generally directing people towards relevant associations, trade fairs and publications: www.uktradeinvest.gov.uk

A network of Chambers of Commerce in Spain offers a variety of information-based services to the potential entrepreneur. They will be able to give advice on all aspects of business creation, from the types of legal entity that can be formed to the different incentives available locally for business creation. The Chambers will also help to research a market prior to making a business plan. Usually these services are completely free. Some Chambers include a *Ventanilla Unica Empresarial*, a system of guiding a prospective business person through the processes involved in incorporating and registering a business.

Launched by the Ministry of Public Administrations (www.map.es), the network of *Ventanillas Unicas Empresariales* (One-Stop Shops for Businesses) has created an integrated system providing future entrepreneurs with information and advice on the formalities required to start up a business. What makes this service so innovative is that all the facilities for setting up a business are provided in a single location, albeit in the Spanish language. Visitors to a *Ventanilla Unica* go through three separate phases.

- **Information and guidance**. Entrepreneurs are pointed in the right direction, based on their requirements and provided with basic information on starting a business.

- **Advice**. A personal advisor then studies a business plan and, following a personal interview, gives an assessment of the project and a range of alternatives. Advisors provide entrepreneurs with information regarding the suitable legal form for their business, labour obligations, private financing and government aid.

- **Formalities**. Suitable projects are then forwarded to the procedure management centre. Here the officer-in-charge, in close co-operation with representatives of the tax and social security authorities and the regional and local authorities, will co-ordinate all of the procedures needed to set up the business such as obtaining municipal licences, dealing with fiscal obligations, labour and social security obligations.

POPULAR BUSINESSES

Bars, cafés and restaurants

Many people dream of running a bar or a restaurant in the sun. Some have been successful, but for every successful catering establishment there are many more that have ruined their owners. Competition is fierce. The hours, especially in the height of the tourist season, are very long. A normal bar or restaurant in the summer months will be open until the small hours of the morning and then be open again for lunch the next day, seven days a week. In peak season it cannot close for even a day since customers go elsewhere. A catering business also suffers from world events, disasters, climate and the economy.

Computer sales and service

While most people use computers few know what to do when problems arise. We need an English speaking expert to sort it out, someone to help us stop our computer crashing, get our email running smoothly again and somewhere to buy our bits and pieces including user-friendly English language software. Anyone skilled in graphic design can also find a niche for web design and short-run print work – advertising, posters, banners, flyers, programmes, menus, invitations, etc.

Construction work

Painting and decorating, plumbing, building, carpentry and similar skills are in demand from ex-pats who want to use the services of tradesmen to whom they can describe the required task without any language problems. Many offer their services as part of the 'black economy' and are paid in cash. However, moving into large contracts will mean dealing with a different customer base – people who want *IVA* receipts to reduce their liability for income tax.

Estate agents

Opening an estate agency business is easy. Unlike many other European countries the estate agency market in Spain is not governed by regulations. There are many people working in Spain in real estate without any background or qualifications although some are registered through a professional association. A booming property market means a very good standard of living. On the debit side it is a results orientated business, with a hard-sell approach and a despised reputation.

Hairdressing

Good hairdressing and beauty saloons flourish. Women go to a hairdresser on a regular basis, preferably to one where they can at least chat to the operator. Hairdressers with additional beauty treatment have an advantage. Independent, mobile hairdressers can also make a good living. English barbers rarely exist – yet men need to talk as much as women.

Hotels, guesthouses and B&Bs

This is yet another area where people dream of having a successful business in the sun. With a good establishment, in a good location, look at a capital cost of one million euros. Too much? Compromise on location by going to the country and renovating a ruin! This is only one downside. Income in a well modernised premises is only 50€ per night for a double room. The holiday season is short, so the room-occupancy rate is only 25 per cent over the year. Most visitors to the coast will rent an apartment or stay in a budget hotel on a package holiday. Guesthouse and B&B demand is mainly for independent travellers in the inland areas where it would be unusual for guests to stay more than two or three days before moving on. That is unless the location had something really special to offer.

Kennels and catteries

While finding the right premises may be difficult, demand is high. If someone wishes to go on holiday, or back to the UK to visit friends and family – where does the dog or cat go? People who live in Spain welcome a good English run kennel or cattery for their animals, not a Spanish owned one, as they treat their animals differently! Opening a kennel or cattery means a place in the country but a word of caution. Just because a person has bought land in the country it does not give them a right to open a business. Planning permission is necessary.

Property management

This covers property cleaning, pool maintenance and gardening. This is relatively low paid, unskilled and seasonal but if correctly managed can be a successful business.

Satellite television installation

This is one business where there is little Spanish competition – the language barrier in reverse. Demand for English language TV is high – or to be more direct, demand for a SKY package is high. While new urbanisations and apartments have communal satellite receivers, there is a demand from owners of individual properties.

Shops and boutiques

Selling the right product in the right area can be very successful. Examples are a flower shop, an English bookshop, a butcher, a small supermarket with British products and a second-hand furniture shop.

WORKING ON YOUR OWN ACCOUNT

A European Union national

European Union nationals can now work in Spain without any restriction. They can work under the same conditions as Spaniards, the only thing they are required to do is to obtain their residence card.

A non-EU foreigner

Non-EU autonomous workers must have the required residence permit and work permit. Non-EU residents in Spain with a work permit and an employment contract cannot re-establish themselves to work on their own account until they obtain a corresponding work permit.

NEW OR EXISTING BUSINESS?

Buying an existing business

It is easier to buy an existing business than it is to start a new one. Taking over an established business is less of a risk than starting something new. Buying an existing business that is profitable is not easy. Most people do not sell a thriving business without a good reason. Traditional Spanish businesses are usually passed down within the family.

- What is the reason for selling? Is there a hidden motive?

- Check at the local planning office for any development that may affect a business.

- Have two independent valuations been obtained?

- Make sure sales turnover and profit claims can be substantiated while accepting that the declared turnover for tax purposes is usually lower than actual turnover.

- Remember when buying a business property in Spain that all debts against the property are automatically transferred to the new owner.

- It is important to obtain all necessary licences and approvals before signing any lease or purchase contract, or alternatively such leases and contracts should be signed subject to the licences and approvals being obtained.

- Never sign anything that is not fully understood.

Starting a new business

What type of company?

A self-employed person *(trabajador autónomo)* or a sole trader *(empresa individual)* does not have the protection of a limited company should the business fail. It may be advantageous to operate as a limited company, but limited companies cannot be purchased off the shelf. A *gestor* can do this, but it usually takes some time.

A business may assume various legal titles. Most small business people operate as sole traders and must register with the appropriate trade association, and pay a small entrance fee and a monthly subscription. They are taxed as an individual. A small company is usually a private limited company *(Sociedad de responsabilidad Limitada)* designated *SL*. It is the simplest and most common form of limited company, does not have any public shares and is subject to corporate taxation. A large limited company is a public company *(Sociedad Anonima)* designated *SA* which is similar to a British plc or an American Inc. Forming an *SA* requires significant share capital, at least 50 employees and one director.

In order to create a new business entity the most important prerequisite is patience. You will have to visit a range of offices and officials. The hurdles are too great for some, so 40 per cent of businesses remain unlicenced. There is little doubt that setting up a company is a specialised task – even for a small *SL*. It is important to appoint someone who has experience in doing it. The core document is a Deed of Incorporation which must be signed before a notary. However, registration of the company name, registration at the tax office and payment of a share capital deposit into a bank account are all necessary before a business is up and running. This, together with an opening licence, all costs money. The minimum cost for setting up a small *SL* is as follows.

Transfer tax	30€
Share capital deposit	3,000€
Company name and registration	200€
Legal fees	1,000€
Opening licence	200€
Total	**4,430€**

Business considerations

- Is there a business plan in existence?

- Most people are too optimistic about the prospects of a new business.

- Lack of capital is the most common reason for business failure.

- All banks are wary of lending to a new business.

- Borrowing money? Is it the euro, the dollar or the pound?

- When starting a retail business, people traffic is governed by location.

- Is access to motorways and rail links important?

- Are any housing developments or new shopping centres planned nearby?

Grants

Investment incentives are available from the Spanish government and the European Union. Incentives include investment subsidies, tax relief, low-interest or interest-free loans, social security rebates and reduced local taxes during the start-up period. There are also regional government incentives for investment in economic promotion zones, declining industrial zones and urgent reindustrialisation zones.

LEASEHOLD OR FREEHOLD

Business premises are most commonly purchased as leasehold because it is easy to terminate the lease if required. Buying freehold (purchasing a property) may be worthwhile for a secure business venture. Some contracts offer leasehold with a view to purchase, which allows the buyer to agree a price with the vendor at the start of a lease.

A Spanish lease is known as a *cesion* (cession) the historic definition *traspaso* (transfer) no longer being appropriate. The landlord owns the shell of the building, for which they receive a fee and a monthly rent, but the tenant owns everything else. The lease can be anything from five to 25 years and sometimes can be for an indefinite period. However, five to ten years is a normal lease period.

Lease agreements have no set formula. The exact terms of the lease are stated in the contract. During the agreed period of the lease, rent can only be increased by the annual cost of living index. The leaseholder is responsible for services such as electricity, water, personal taxes and social security payments. *IBI* may be paid by the landlord.

In the UK a leaseholder is responsible for the full term of the lease regardless of what happens. In Spain only two months' notice are required to terminate a lease. A landlord cannot terminate a lease for any reason other than non-payment of rent.

The cost of a leasehold comprises a one off, up front fee, for which a ten per cent deposit will be required to secure its purchase and the balance usually payable in 30–60 days. The rules are similar to buying a property – should the potential leaseholder default the deposit is lost. Upon completion the landlord must be paid a security deposit of two months' rent and further rent instalments paid monthly in advance. A normal business transfer will cost 1,250€ for legal fees which includes preparation of a new lease contract, licence transfers and census registrations.

The benefits of freehold should not be ignored. The initial cost may be high, but so too is property inflation. The freeholder always has the option of selling the leasehold of a property for which they will receive a fee and monthly rental income. The costs of buying are exactly the same as for buying any property.

LEGAL REQUIREMENTS

Opening licence

A business with premises such as a shop, workshop or offices requires an opening licence (*licencia de apertura*) from the local town hall before starting. For a new building it is necessary to employ the services of an architect, to submit a project to the town hall. The council will visit the premises to make sure that they fulfil all legal and sanitary obligations, but it is not unusual for them to take six months before examining a project and issuing a licence. Many people operate on the basis of a stamped application for a *licencia de apertura*. This is usually tolerated by the authorities.

If a business is likely to inconvenience the local community, such as by noise from a bar or discotheque, the council will insist on certain requirements before granting an opening licence. A licence application is not necessary if the business premises are to be used for the same purpose as previously. The serving of alcohol and food also requires a health licence.

A licence issued for a business owned by a non-EU national may be conditional on the employment of a minimum number of EU citizens. A non-EU citizen wishing to start a business in Spain must also make an investment of around 120,000€ in order to be granted a work permit.

Special authorisation

To be able to carry out certain business activities other relevant authorisation is needed. This will depend on in which sector a company is going to operate. For example, in order to be able to open a bar, restaurant or hotel an authorisation from the Delegation of the General Directorate of Tourism in the Region where the business activity is going to be performed must be obtained. There are also a number of regulated activities which require additional approval, such as travel agencies, security and toxic substances storage.

Building work

When work must be carried out on premises or land where the business activity is going to take place, the relevant Works Licence (*Licencia de Obras*) must be requested from the town hall. Details required include the plans, relevant application form, layout and sketch of the project, description of the works to be carried out and its total valuation.

Declaration of opening a workplace

The opening of the workplace must be declared to the labour authorities – *Declaracion de Apertura del Centro de Trabajo* – within 30 days following the start of a business activity. The official form obtained at the *Direccion Provincial del Ministerio de Trabajo y Seguridad Social* gives information about the company, employees and activity.

Social security

All self-employed people, even those who work part-time, must contribute to the social security system. Not only are social security contributions under this scheme higher than for employees, there are also fewer benefits too. There are various levels of social security payable, depending on the size of pension on retirement and if aged over 50 years. The *autonomo* scheme will cost a minimum of around 230€ per month.

Impuesto sobre Actividades Economicas (*IAE*)

All self-employed people and businesses must register at the *Hacienda* to pay a tax known as *IAE*. It is payable if business turnover exceeds 600,000€ per year. What is it? They say it is a tax on economic activities. The high sales threshold is designed to help small and medium businesses.

Impuesto sobre el Valor Anadido (IVA)

All self-employed people and businesses must register for Valued Added Tax (*IVA*) and levy this tax on all services or goods.

Taxation

Small businesses pay an estimated quarterly tax with a refund made, or an additional payment demanded, at the end of the tax year. Limited companies must file corporate tax returns to the provincial tax headquarters in the area where the business is registered. Various returns must be made including corporation tax, personal income tax and Value Added Tax. Procedures for keeping the books are also defined.

FURTHER INFORMATION

Guy Hobb, *Starting a Business in Spain*. Oxford: Vacation Work Publications. A definitive guide to setting up or buying a business in Spain.

Spanish Embassy, Office for Economic Affairs, 66 Chiltern St, London W1U 4LS. Tel: 0044 2074672330. A starting point for employers.

The British Consulate website www.ukinspain.com is a good starting point for job seekers.

www.Spainlawyer.com is an excellent site for employment law.

www.ipyme.org An office for small and medium enterprises.

14
Understanding Personal Taxation

INTRODUCTION

Spain is no longer the tax haven it once was, when taxes were low and tax evasion a way of life. Today it is more difficult to avoid paying taxes and penalties are severe. However, despite the efforts of the authorities to curb tax dodgers, tax evasion is still widespread. Many non-resident homeowners and foreign residents think that they should be exempt from Spanish taxes. Some inhabit a twilight world, not officially resident in any country. Yet tax evasion is illegal. It is a criminal offence and offenders are heavily fined or even imprisoned. On the other hand, tax avoidance, paying as little tax as possible and finding loopholes in the tax laws, is common. It is not so much the level of taxes, but the number of different taxes, for sometimes small amounts, which makes taxation complex.

This chapter will only deal with personal taxation. A later chapter is devoted to inheritance tax. Business taxation is a totally separate, complex subject outside the scope of this book. To start with, let's look at a list of taxes.

Personal taxation

- **Income tax** (*impuesto sobre la renta de las personas físicas*) is payable by residents on world-wide income and by non-residents on income arising in Spain.

- Non-residents and residents with more than one property must pay a deemed **property income tax** (*rentimientos del capital inmobiliario*) which is usually referred to as *renta.*

- **Wealth tax** (*impuesto sobre el patrimonio*) is payable by residents and non-residents on high-value capital assets, including property.

- **Capital gains tax** (*impuesto sobre incremento de patrimonio de la renta de un bien inmueble*) is payable by both residents and non-residents on the profits made on the sale of property and other assets located in Spain.

- **Inheritance and gift tax** (*impuesto sobre sucesiones y donaciones*) is payable by residents on the transfer of worldwide assets and by non-residents on Spanish assets, upon death.

Business taxation

- **Business tax** (*impuesto sobre actividades economicas*) is paid by all businesses with an annual turnover of more than 600,000€, including self-employed.

- **Company** or **corporation tax** (*impuesto sobre sociedades*).

- **Value added tax** (*impuesto sobre el valor anadido*) is payable on a wide range of goods and services at varying rates.

Other taxes

- **Property tax** (*impuesto sobre bienes inmeubles – IBI*) is paid by all property owners to the town hall, whether resident or non-resident.

- Taxes concerned with buying a property, including **transfer tax** (*derechos reales*) and **land tax** (*plus valia*).

- **Offshore company tax** (*impuesto especial*) is an annual tax on offshore companies which do not name an individual owner of the property, or the source of investment.

- **Waste collection** (*basura*) is an annual tax payable in some areas, whether resident or non-resident.

- **Motor vehicle tax** (*impuesto de circulacion*) is paid annually by all those owning a Spanish registered vehicle, plus a one-off **registration tax** upon purchase.

PRINCIPAL FACTS

Taxation is at the best of times complicated. In that context the Spanish taxman does not disappoint. As you would expect, the tax system is also ever changing. Most taxes in Spain are based on self-assessment where the individual is liable to report and calculate any tax due. The *Agenda Estatal de Administración Tributaria* collects government taxes but it is commonly called by its old name, *Hacienda*. The Spanish tax year is 1 January to 31 December. Tax returns must be presented between 1 May and the 20 June. Tax is paid at the same time as its declaration in June, or 60 per cent with the balance by the following November. Tax returns are submitted to the district office where a person is resident for tax purposes, or they can be filed and payment made at designated banks. Payment must be made in cash as personal cheques are not accepted, although if filing at a bank where an account is held, they will make a transfer to the tax authorities – the preferred method. If no payment is due on a declaration, it still must be filed at the tax office in the normal way. Delay in filing a tax return may result in a surcharge while late payment of a tax bill will result in a surcharge of 20 per cent. Copies of tax returns should be retained for five years.

Getting advice

Since we have difficulties with tax at the best of times, the average new resident or non-resident, grappling with the language of tax authorities, has little chance of getting a declaration correct. Enter the *asesor fiscal* who will not only perform these administrative tasks but may even suggest legitimate methods of tax avoidance. It is not essential to have fiscal representative but if you own more than one property, or a commercial property, or for a foreign company owning a property in Spain, it is really necessary to have one. Fiscal representation is cheap, about 50€ per year for one person. For the relatively small cost involved, most people are usually better off employing a fiscal representative to handle their tax affairs rather than doing it themselves.

It is possible to obtain free tax advice from the information section at the local tax office where staff will answer queries and assist in completing a tax declaration via their PADRE computer system. Some offices have staff who speak English and other foreign languages. An alternative is to present details direct to a bank that in many cases has PADRE forms on its computer. Most *asesor fiscal* use the PADRE program as well.

Who pays what

A non-resident spends less than six months per year in Spain. A Spanish resident is one who spends more than six months per year in the country, who has a *residencia* and has notified the tax authorities back home of their departure on form P85. This triggers entry into the Spanish tax system, which has a treaty with other European countries designed to ensure income which has already been taxed in one country is not taxed again in another country. Spanish residents are taxed on their worldwide income, whereas non-residents are taxed in Spain only on income arising in Spain, which is exempt from tax in their home country.

There are two important points – firstly there is a five-year limitation on the collection of back taxes. If no action has been taken during this period to collect unpaid tax, it cannot be collected. Secondly, UK government pensions (eg. police, fire, government officials) are taxed in the UK and not in Spain.

Documentation

To complete tax returns, some documentation is necessary.

- Personal details: *NIE, residencia* number, address, age and marital status (the Family Book).

- Proof of income.

- A year-end bank statement showing any interest received and average balance. The interest is added to income and the average balance is part of the worldwide assets for wealth tax.

- A recent *IBI* receipt which will contain a property value (*valor catastral*) which is used to calculate *renta* tax.

- Receipts for tax paid in another country.

- Details of any changes in stocks, shares, investments or insurance policies.

- Details of any changes in major assets such as property, boats and artifacts.

- Proof to claim any deductions.

INCOME TAX

It is not necessary to file a tax return if your income is less then 8,000€ a year. This applies to married couples and retired people too. The only condition is that no more than 1,600€ of this income is from investments. A salaried worker earning less than 22,000€ probably does not need to make a tax declaration. This does not mean non-payment of income tax. It means that their withholding tax, taken out of their salary during the year, has been carefully calculated to match their liability. The tax office recalculates their final tax bill and makes any refund.

There are four steps to determine tax liability.

1 Calculate gross income.

2 Deduct allowances.

3 Apply tax rates.

4 Deduct further allowances.

Calculating gross income

Income tax is payable on both earned and unearned income. Taxable income includes salaries, fees, pensions, capital gains for residents, letting income, dividends and interest payments. It also includes employee benefits such as profit sharing plans, bonuses, company car, payment in kind, stock options and children's private education. And of course for a non-resident or a resident with more than one property it also includes *renta* (see later).

Deducting allowances

The following deductions can be made from gross income:

- all social security payments;

- a personal allowance;

- a deduction from income – a wage earner allowance;

- an allowance if unemployed and accepted a job in different locality;

- a disability allowance;

- a dependant's allowance;

- professional and trade union fees;

- Spanish company pension contributions;

- a percentage of an annuity;

- child-support payments made as a result of a court decision;

- maintenance payments as the result of a court order;

- legal expenses;

- 60 per cent of any dividends.

Applying tax rates

Income tax rates for individuals start at 15 per cent on taxable income up to 4,000€ and rise to 45 per cent on taxable income above 45,000€. Tax payments are allocated between the Spanish state (85 per cent) and the autonomous regions (15 per cent), although some autonomous regions, e.g. the Basque Country, Catalonia and La Rioja, offer reductions in their apportionment. The table below demonstrates the combined tax payable.

Taxable income €	Tax rate %	Cumulative tax €
Up to 4,000	15	600
4,000 to 13,800	24	2,952
13,800 to 25,800	28	6,312
25,800 to 45,000	37	13,416
Over 45,000	45	

Deducting further allowances

After calculating gross income, applying deductions, and calculating tax due from the percentage table above, and before arriving at a final tax bill, certain other deductions can be made. They have a dramatic effect on a tax bill as they are applied on a net figure. You can deduct these other allowances:

- personal income tax paid in another country against the double taxation treaty;

- 15 per cent of the cost of the purchase or renovation of a principal residence but excluding additions such as a garage, swimming pool or normal maintenance;

- deductions for mortgage payments – capital plus interest;

- 20 per cent of the value of donations to charities;

- 15 per cent of the amount invested in a mortgage savings account;

- ten per cent of life premiums or premiums for an invalidity policy;

- 75 per cent of any *plus valia* tax paid as a result of a property sale.

Example

Let's focus on a retired couple now resident in Spain. They have owned their property for a few years and have carried out no alterations during the current tax year. She has a state pension from the UK. He has earnings of 29,200€ from various sources but mainly occupational pension schemes and investments. Income tax liability is simple to calculate.

She pays no tax at all and is not required to make a declaration as her earnings are under 8,000€ per year.

He will have a personal allowance of 3,400€ deducted from gross income (4,200€ if over 65 years). Taxable income of 25,800€ at 28 per cent will result in a tax bill of 6,312€ as there are no further deductions or allowances.

RENTA

A property owner's tax on deemed letting income (*rendimientos del capital inmobiliario*) is usually referred to as *renta*. *Renta* is nothing to do with renting out a property and nothing to do with *IBI* either.

All non-resident property owners or residents owning more than one property in Spain are deemed to receive an income of two per cent of the fiscal value (*valor castral*) of their property or 1.1 per cent if the fiscal value has been revised since 1 January 1994. Non-residents pay a flat rate tax of 25 per cent on this income. A property valued at 100,000€, at a tax rate of 1.1 per cent, will have a liability of 275€. It should be noted that the valuation in the *valor castral* will be about 50 per cent of the market value. The example above is effectively for a property with a market value of 200,000€.

In the case of residents there is no deduction, but residents who own more than one property will be subject to tax on their second home. In this case the *renta* is added as income for income tax purposes. In the example above 1,100€ is added as income as if it were more earnings. This means they pay tax on this at their normal income tax rate. At the lowest tax rate of 15 per cent the bill is 165€ which can be split in two if the second property is jointly owned.

WEALTH TAX

Impuesto extraordinario sobre el patrimonio is referred to simply as *patrimonio*. It applies to both residents and non-residents but wealth tax affects each group differently. A resident is required to declare their worldwide assets while a non-resident declares only their property and assets in Spain.

Wealth is calculated by totalling all assets and deducting all liabilities. Assets include property, car, boat, business, value of Spanish bank balances, life insurance, jewellery, stocks, shares and bonds. The value of property is the highest of purchase price, fiscal value or a value assessed by the authorities. Deductions are made for mortgages, debts, the vested rights in pension plans, and any wealth tax paid in another country.

Residents are entitled to a general allowance of 108,000€ per person for all assets, plus an additional allowance of 150,000€ per person for a main residence, making a total wealth tax allowance of 258,000€ per person. If the property is held in joint names each person is entitled to claim the exemption. There is no allowance for non-residents, who must pay wealth tax on all their assets in Spain, which for most people will consist only of their home.

After the allowance has been deducted (or not in the case of non-residents) wealth, defined as assets less liabilities per person, is taxed at a sliding scale beginning at 0.2 per cent. A non-resident owner with a property of market value 200,000€ will pay 436€, or 218€ each for joint owners. A resident with a single property valued at 200,000€ will pay no tax.

Wealth up to €	Tax rate %	Cumulative tax €
167,000	0.2	338
334,000	0.3	839
716,000	0.5	2,751
1,337,00	0.9	8,335

Property tax

Many people view *renta* tax and wealth tax as one item, calling it *renta* and *patrimonio*, or even calling them a property tax. In the case of a non-resident, taking the example of a property with a market value of 200,000€, *renta* tax is 275€ and *patrimonio* tax is 436€, i.e. a total of 701€ per year for having a property in Spain (plus of course *IBI* and any community charges).

CAPITAL GAINS TAX

Liability to capital gains tax applies to residents and non-residents. Capital gains tax is payable on a profit from the sale of assets such as property, stocks and shares, antiques, art and jewellery. Since most ex-pats will have arranged their investments free of tax and non-residents will only have a property, capital gains in practice should only apply to the sale of a property. A capital gain is based on the difference between the purchase price and the selling price of a property, as stated in the *escritura*, less the cost of buying and selling.

Exemptions

Residents aged over 65 are exempt from the profit made from the sale of their principal home, irrespective of how long they have owned it.

Residents aged below 65 are exempt from CGT on their principal home, provided they've lived there for at least three years and plan to buy another home in Spain within three years of the sale.

For both residents and non-residents, a property purchased before 31 December 1986 is free of CGT.

Persons over 65 who contract to sell their principal residence in exchange for a lifetime right to inhabit the dwelling, along with a monthly payment – an equity release scheme – are free from CGT.

Tax rates

Non-residents are taxed at a flat rate of 35 per cent. Buyers from non-resident property sellers are required to withhold five per cent of the total purchase price and pay it direct to the tax authorities, making sure a seller is in part covered for CGT. Capital gains made by residents are treated as income and taxed in the year in which the gain was made, at a maximum tax rate of 15 per cent.

Taxable gain calculation

1. Take the original purchase price entered in the *escritura* and add all official expenses occurred in purchasing the property, which we know will be about ten per cent of the purchase price.

2. Increase the value above by the official inflation occurring between the time of sale and time of purchase. The Spanish government maintains official inflation statistics. So if the time between sale and purchase was six years and the official inflation in the same period was 12 per cent then the value above is increased by the inflation factor of 1.12.

3. Take the selling price in the *escritura* and reduce it for any selling expenses such as estate agents' commissions.

4. Subtract 2 from 3 above to establish the capital gain which is taxed accordingly.

Additional reduction for buyers between 1987 and 1994

Property owners in this category have the right to an additional 11 per cent reduction per year. So if a property was bought in 1990 the tax liability above is reduced by a further 44 per cent.

Examples

Let us take a non-resident purchasing a property in 1997 for 100,000€ and selling it six years later for 200,000€. Inflation is 12 per cent, purchasing on costs ten per cent and estate agents' commission ten per cent on selling.

Purchase price	100,000€
Add cost of purchase	10,000€
Sub total	110,000€
Add inflation @ 12 per cent	14,500€
(A) Sub total	124,500€
Selling price	200,000€
Less costs of selling	20,000€
(B) Sub total	180,000€
Capital gain	B – A = 55,500€
Tax @35 per cent	19,500€

A resident will have the gain added to earnings for income tax. Taxed at a lower rate of 15 per cent the total liability is 8,300€.

AUTHOR'S NOTE

Tax tables are boring. They have not been used in this chapter or in any other chapters of this book. Rounded extracts from tax tables have been used. This aids understanding, but suffers in that an example may marginally differ from the real thing. Tax tables are altered annually too! So treat these examples with a degree of caution.

Declaring a tax liability is also depressing. Filling out forms in Spanish is not everyone's idea of fun. The difficulty of doing this can be completely avoided by following my recommendation of using an *asesor fiscal*. It costs very little. For this reason no details of tax declaration procedures, or the various declaration forms, have been given.

15
On the Road

INTRODUCTION

In recent years major motorway construction covering over 8,000km has been completed. They can be spectacular roads passing through mountains, across valleys, rivers or ravines. Madrid is now connected to all its provincial capitals by fast road communication and it is also possible to drive from France to Gibraltar by motorway. It fact it will soon be possible to drive by motorway from Perth in Scotland to Lisbon in Portugal through France and Spain. Some of the newer motorways are toll roads (*autopistas de peajes*) which can be expensive.

Driving is still an enjoyable experience in many rural areas (outside the Spanish holiday time of August) when it is possible to drive for hours without seeing another motorist. Driving in Spain's major cities such as Madrid and Barcelona is no different from other major cities in Europe and not for the faint-hearted.

Unfortunately Spain has one of the worst accident records in Europe with over 5,500 deaths and over 1.6 million accidents per annum. Around 40 per cent of fatal accidents involve drivers over the alcohol limit. Spanish motorists do drive ridiculously fast.

ROADS

Spain's motorways are known as *autopistas* (A roads) or *autovias* (E for European roads). Both are characterised by distinctive blue signposting. *Autopistas* are toll roads found on some short sections of motorway which have been built by commercial contractors or for expensive shortcuts over difficult terrain.

Other major roads in Spain are identified by the sign *red de carreteras del estado* (state road network) being *carreteras nacionales* and signified by the letter N on maps. These roads tend to be busy, single lane roads, often taking traffic more suited to toll roads. Secondary routes are the narrower *carreteras comarcales* (letter C) and minor roads, *carretera autonomica,* are denoted by the initials of the province followed by a number.

On major roads each kilometre is marked with a number showing the distance from Madrid or, in the case of provinces, from a provincial capital. These kilometre markers are often used as convenient meeting points, to establish the location of a building or even a postal address.

The speed limits are:

- *autopistas*   120 km/h

- *autovias*   120 km/h

- *carreteras nacionale*   90 km/h

- *carreteras comarcales* 60 km/h

- *carreteras autonomica* 50 km/h, or as signposted

DRIVING DIFFERENCES

The most obvious differences are of course left-hand drive cars and driving on the right-hand side of the road. There are other differences:

- Going around roundabouts in an anti-clockwise direction.

- If you find you are going in the wrong direction on a motorway, you can go back the other way when the sign *cambio de sentido* appears.

- When trying to turn left on a busy road, it may be necessary to turn right first and then cross the carriageway.

- The sequence of traffic lights (*semaforos*) is red, green, amber and back to red.

- Two flashing amber lights means 'slow down, danger ahead'.

- Respect the narrow inside lane, it is for scooters.

- All vehicle documents (or copies) such as insurance details, car registration and technical *ITV* sheets (see later) should be kept in a car for inspection by police if so required.

- Motorists must carry two approved red warning triangles, a full set of spare bulbs and fuses and a reflective vest. It is advisable (but not mandatory) to carry a fire extinguisher and a first-aid kit.

One pleasing difference is the cost of fuel. *Gasolina* (petrol), *gasoleo* (diesel) and *gasolina sin plomo* (unleaded petrol) are available everywhere at prices 35 per cent below the most expensive European price. The number of filling stations is increasing rapidly. They also sell newspapers, food and snacks.

Motorway services vary in standard and frequency. On new *autovias* they are of a high standard open 24 hours per day. On older roads the unsuspecting driver will be directed to a town or village where fuel, food, toilets and sometimes beds are available.

PURCHASING A NEW CAR (*EL COCHE*)

The market for purchasing new cars is similar across Europe. Large dealers sell new and some secondhand cars at competitive prices with a good after-sales service. Since all dealerships are monitored by car manufacturers their service is efficient, well organised and, above all, reputable.

Given Spain's geographical location and the presence of large car manufacturing plants in Valencia, the popular brands are Seat and Ford. French products come next.

Quality German cars are always popular and the market penetration of small Far Eastern cars is high. New cars are more expensive in Spain than in many other EU countries but they depreciate at a slower rate. Spanish-made cars are generally cheaper than imported cars due to tax differentials.

When purchasing either a new, or secondhand, car documentation is necessary. Some of the following is certainly asked for:

- an *NIF*;

- a *residencia* or passport;

- a copy of an *escritura* for a home owned in Spain or a property rental contract of one year's duration;

- a *certificado de empadronamiento*;

- a recognised driving licence, which in the case of a non-resident should be an International Licence.

Cost of a new car

Details of the cost of a small to medium sized family diesel estate car are given below. The normal specification for quotation includes radio, air conditioning and metallic paint plus of course the engine type. Quotations are always given for a total cost to include all taxes and charges. Registration tax can vary according to the engine type and size – if the engine is less than 1600 cc or a diesel under 2000 cc the tax is seven per cent, over that the tax is 12 per cent. When buying a new car from a dealer it will be registered as part of the deal. The registration certificate is called the *permiso de circulacion*, which is proof of ownership. Any part exchange is credited separately. In the example below the various taxes and fees account for 25 per cent of a new car's cost. Payment of a car may be phased, not by hire purchase but by a system of *letras* (bill of exchange), details of which are outlined in Chapter 4.

Basic list price	14,776€
Special offer discount	1,300€
Net cost	13,476€
IVA at 16%	2,155€
Total net cost	15,631€
Extra on road charges	
Impuesto de matriculation 7% (registration tax)	979€
Matriculation (registration) certificate	260€
Seguridad mechanica (extra guarantee)	240€
Impuesto municipal (road tax for one year)	80€
Sub total	1,559€
TOTAL COST	**17,190€**

PURCHASING A USED CAR

Regrettably the secondhand car market does not enjoy a good reputation, with the usual unsavoury dealers in evidence, some of whom are British. Fortunately the quality of a modern secondhand car is high. It is price, poor administration, lack of customer service and dishonesty which gives this market its poor reputation. The Spanish market for secondhand cars is unusual as a large number of year-old rental cars, with relatively low mileage, are sold through secondhand outlets. Trade-ins from new sales dealerships are also sold through second hand outlets. Again, when buying a used car from a dealer, registration will form part of the deal.

There is yet another market for used cars – those sold through small ads in weekly newspapers. For first-time buyers in Spain the advice is to tread carefully. The risk of a poor product or incorrect paperwork is too great. A simple agreement should be drawn up to sell a car privately. It should contain factual details of the buyer, the seller, and details of the car, price and form of payment, the date and appropriate signatures. This is good practice. A proof of sale should be stamped at *Jefatura Provincial de Trafico* to exempt the seller from future fines, accidents or taxes which the buyer may incur.

CAR REGISTRATION

Plates

Spanish registration plates consist of four digits followed by three letters. It is no longer possible to tell where the car is from, or its age, from the number plate. However, there are still many cars on the road with an old style registration plate which consists of one or two letters denoting the province where the vehicle is registered followed by four digits and two more letters indicating the age of the car.

The original registration remains permanently with a car unless it is re-registered. If buying a secondhand car in Spain, it's best to buy one with the new style registration or one registered in the province where you live.

The vehicle registration document is in two parts. One is for details of the car and one for details of the owner. The details of the car do not alter, whereas the section giving details of the owner will each time there is a change.

Transfer of ownership

When a secondhand car is purchased from a private individual it will need to be registered within ten days of purchase. When selling a car privately it is important to ensure the transfer is completed correctly by the new owner. Rather like debts on a property, as long as the previous owner is still registered they are liable for any parking tickets, road tax and accident claims.

It is a procedure for which many people use a *gestor* as a visit to a provincial capital and the infamous *Jefatura Provincial de Trafico* office is necessary. This Spanish department has a reputation for being difficult with complex procedures. It is the worst example of Spanish bureaucracy. However if you are selling and wish to 'do it yourself' here is how. Obtain a form entitled *Notificacion de Transferencia de Vehiculos* from the *Jefatura Provincial de Trafico*, at the *Vehiculos* counter. Complete it and present it with the following:

- A mutually signed bill of sale including the price paid, the car's kilometre reading, the present condition (as seen) without a guarantee (*sin garantia*).

- The *Permiso de Circulacion* with the transfer of owner's and the seller's signature completed.

- The current year's paid up municipal vehicle tax receipt and a photocopy.

- If appropriate the current *Inspección Tecnica de Vehiculos* (*ITV*).

- A receipt for the payment of vehicle transfer tax, paid to the *Hacienda* at four per cent of the fiscal value.

- Proof of identity.

- Payment of a fee of around 45€.

- A stamped, self-addressed envelope so that the traffic authorities can send the registration document to the new owner.

Transfer tax

A transfer tax called *Impuesto Sobre Transmisiones Patrimoniales y Actos Juridicos Documentados* which is four per cent of the fiscal value is levied on the sale of a secondhand car. The fiscal value of a new car is decided by the tax office. The fiscal value is reduced each year until it is ten years old, when it is reduced to ten per cent of the new value. The tax is the responsibility of the buyer, but as the seller actually pays it, most sellers include the tax in the sales price. This tax is declared on form *compraventa de vehiculos usados entre particulares* obtained from the *Hacienda* and paid within 30 days of selling to the provincial tax office of the regional government.

Deregistering

Deregistering a car is called *baja de matricula*. This form is again obtained from *Trafico* and must have attached a receipt for the current year's municipal vehicle tax. It can be used when scrapping an old vehicle, or if a vehicle is stolen. As an incentive to encourage scrapping an old car, the government will reduce registration tax by 480€ to 720€ upon buying a new one.

CAR IMPORT AND EXPORT

Six-month temporary stay

Genuine tourists and visitors are permitted to bring a foreign registered car to Spain, but it is not permitted to stay for longer than six months in any one year. Driving a foreign registered car temporarily in Spain requires appropriate insurance, a national identity sticker on the back of the car, two red triangles, spare bulbs, a reflective vest and a first-aid kit. The headlights need to be adjusted. In the case of an accident the insurance certificate, the drivers' licence and a passport need to be kept handy. Permanently driving a right-hand drive car in Spain is not a good idea but if kept for more than six months in any year it should be tested and re-registered as a Spanish car.

This six-month period is based on the stay of the person rather than the stay of the car. The six months is the length a tourist can stay. A car can remain in Spain more than six months, but it cannot be legally driven. It is of course common knowledge that many citizens of other EU countries live full-time in Spain without obtaining a residence card and still operate their cars with foreign plates. While the police may turn a blind eye to the movement of EU citizens, foreign plated cars are viewed as a safety hazard since they have no regular MOT.

Spanish residents importing a car

There is a bewildering and ever-changing set of regulations covering the importation of cars. The motorist is seeking cost advantage by using cross-border purchasing and conversely European governments are seeking to block tax loopholes by equalising European law. A simplified approach to the issue goes like this.

- A new resident of Spain wishing to import a vehicle bought six months previously, with taxes paid in another EU country, can do so without any further tax charges.

- A vehicle bought tax-free in another EU country will require the payment of 16 per cent *IVA* on arrival in Spain plus the appropriate registration tax.

- A vehicle bought tax-free outside the EU will require the payment of 16 per cent

IVA, the appropriate registration tax and a further import duty of ten per cent making a whacking 38 per cent for a car over 2000 cc.

It is a costly and complex procedure to import a car, involving proof of tax payment or otherwise and the cost of re-registering the vehicle in Spain. But for a new resident it brings the legislation for importing cars broadly in line with the regulations for importing household effects.

For those seeking commercial advantage, the price of cheaper premium cars available in Holland, Belgium and Germany requires to be balanced against a Spanish re-registration cost of around 700€. In the UK the vehicle's registration document should be surrendered to the DVLA and a Certificate of Permanent Export obtained from them for presentation in Spain. The Spanish authorities will need a certificate (*Certificado de Baja*), issued by the British Consulate, to the effect that the owner has left the UK and intends to reside permanently in Spain.

Homologation is a name given to a procedure where imported vehicles must comply with Spanish safety standards before they can be registered. This is not necessary for vehicles manufactured in the EU. However, a vehicle imported from outside the EU must still undergo homologation and be certified by the manufacturer before it can be registered in Spain.

Non-EU citizens 'sealing' a car

Non-EU citizens can avail themselves of the strange practice of 'sealing' where they can keep a foreign registered car permanently in Spain but only use it for six months in any year, having it sealed by customs officials for the other six months. The sealing is done by the Guardia Civil who put tape across the steering wheel designed to ensure it is not used. It is a useful procedure for people who wish to keep their foreign registered car in Spain all year for use during short regular visits.

Non-resident, non-EU citizens with tourist plates

A tourist can purchase a new car just as easily as purchasing a new shirt. An exact definition is a non-resident, purchasing a car on tourist plates, which is an export registration available in a number of countries. It is called *Matricula Turistica*. The cost is less purchase taxes but not road taxes. The car can be driven for six months and then exported to the tourist's home country of residence where appropriate taxes are then paid. This can only be beneficial if the purchase price in Spain and the tax regime back home are significantly lower than a total purchasing package back home.

It is also possible for non-residents to purchase a vehicle on tourist plates and renew them indefinitely. There is an annual fee for the renewal of tourist plates and of course the car can only be driven six months in a year.

Non-resident, EU citizens with tourist plates

A non-resident, EU citizen can also purchase a car on tourist plate. This time it is with *IVA* but no registration tax. It can be kept indefinitely in Spain but the six month rule applies. It's bewildering!

DOCUMENTATION

Driving licence (*Permiso de Conducir*)

A tourist visiting Spain and driving either their own car or a Spanish rental car can do so with a licence issued in their home country. An international licence also issued in their home country would be better as the standard format can be more easily identified by the authorities.

Since 1996 a Spanish resident from another EU country can drive in Spain with their original, home country licence for as long as it is valid, with no obligation to take out a Spanish licence. However if the holder is a resident in Spain and not opting to obtain a Spanish driving licence, it is still legally necessary to present their UK licence to the *Jefatura Provincial de Trafico* for its details to be entered on their computer.

However as the licence has an old address for a new resident of Spain it is better to exchange it for a Spanish driving licence. If anything goes wrong it makes life just that little bit easier. It can reduce problems at roadside checks.

To exchange a UK licence for a Spanish licence:

- Go to the information counter at the provincial traffic department (*Jefatura Provincial de Trafico*) with the UK licence.

- Complete an appropriate form (*Solicitud de Carnet del Permiso de Conducir*) and present a residency card, a photocopy, the old driving licence and three passport style photographs.

- The new licence is not for life. It is renewable every few years according to age, every five years for those aged 45 to 70 years, every two years for those over 70 years. An embarrassingly simple medical examination is necessary, which is carried out at an approved centre, lasts one and a half minutes and costs 35€.

Since 2004 holders of EU photo card driving licences can drive legally in Spain without the need to register or exchange that licence. If the licence bears a previous UK address, drivers should always carry proof of their residence in Spain when they have lived in the country for more than six months.

The situation for a non-EU citizen resident in Spain presents no ambiguity. The requirement is a Spanish driving licence and nothing else but a Spanish driving licence. A home country licence cannot be exchanged for a Spanish one. Or to put it another way a non-EU licence cannot be exchanged for an EU licence. The net result of all this means non-EU citizens must take a Spanish driving examination, both written and practical, in Spanish, and to do it they have no option but to attend an approved Spanish driving school. An expensive business!

There is no licence penalty point system in Spain for traffic offences, although licences can be suspended for periods from three months to one year depending on the type of offence.

Road tax

All Spanish registered vehicles are liable for road tax (*impuesto municipal sobre vehiculos de traccion mechanica*). The tax is based on *potencia fiscal* – the horsepower of the car. Tax levels are set by individual municipalities and can vary from place to place, with Barcelona the highest. Budget around 160€ per year for a small family sized car. Payment is at the local town hall, or to a subcontracted collection agency such as *SUMA*, during a published time window after which a surcharge is applied. Unlike many other countries a tax disc is not placed inside the windscreen. Some people have avoided paying this tax for years but it catches up with them, complete with fines, when a copy of the last receipt is required upon selling or scrapping a car, which incidentally is an explanation of why many abandoned vehicles litter the countryside.

ITV (technical inspection of vehicles)

After four years a biannual vehicle inspection, known as an *ITV*, is necessary. It is the equivalent of an MOT in the UK. When a car is passed, a sticker is placed inside the windscreen. After ten years it is an annual inspection. If a vehicle fails a test, 15 days are allowed to have it repaired and retested.

The *ITV* test is only valid for vehicles registered in Spain. It has no value in other EU countries. A car registered in another EU country must be tested in accordance with the laws of the country where it is registered.

ACCIDENTS

Unfortunately Spain has one of the highest road accident rates in Europe. A high incidence of foreign drivers is one significant reason. Speed and alcohol are other major reasons. Spanish drivers are similar to the Italians and French – they all drive in a fast, aggressive manner. At slip roads, where they join major roads, no quarter is given or asked by the incoming drivers. Their judgment of speed, slipping into a small gap between moving traffic, can be quite frightening. Trained on 49cc motor scooters, graduating to 125cc motor cycles, Spanish car drivers must overtake immediately, irrespective of speed limits or traffic conditions. Damaged wing mirrors tell of a failure to drive through small gaps.

A 'normal' Spanish car has scratched bumpers. Nothing is more frustrating than the constant bumps a car is subjected to in parking lots. There is a total disregard for the wellbeing of someone else's vehicle. For Spanish drivers, it seems bumpers are designed to be scratched.

For new drivers in Spain it is best to regard all drivers as totally unpredictable and drive cautiously.

Drinking and driving

Despite the high accident rate, drunken driving does not create the same social stigma as it does in many other European countries. Random breath tests can be carried out by the police at any time. Motorists who are involved in accidents, or who infringe motoring regulations, are routinely given alcohol and drug tests. The limit is low – when blood alcohol concentration exceeds 25mg of alcohol per 100ml of blood (15mg for drivers with less than two years' experience or professional drivers) which is about two glasses of wine taken with some food. Drunken driving can result in a fine of up to 602€, suspension of a driving licence and even imprisonment up to six months. Drivers who refuse to take a breath test are liable to a prison sentence of six months to one year. In either case a period of community service may be an alternative to a jail sentence. An accident while under the influence of alcohol can result in an insurance being immediately suspended, meaning the non-payment of repairs, medical expenses and other damages.

CAR INSURANCE

Visitors to Spain for a short-term tourist stay and driving a foreign registered car require insurance. This is a green card, as the international insurance certificate is known. Conversely visitors to the UK driving a Spanish registered car will also require a green card. In the UK a green card is requested from an insurance company, while in Spain it is automatically issued with an annual certificate. Since there are no longer any border posts a green card is really a notification to the insurance company of travel abroad rather than a permit to enter a country.

Spanish law, like that in all other EU countries, demands that all vehicles be fully insured for minimum third-party damage. Basic types of car insurance are available similar to those in the UK. There are some notable differences, both positive and negative. For example vehicle recovery in the event of breakdown is normally covered but protection for passengers may be an extra charge.

Many UK companies operate in the car insurance market. It is therefore quite easy to obtain car insurance by phone and in English. Understanding the type of cover and possible extras presents little difficulty. Car insurance is relatively cheap around 450€ per year for a new car, fully comprehensive, off road parking, four years' no claims for a middle aged driver, a small exclusion for the first part of a claim, breakdown cover and any other driver approved by the insured.

- *Responsabilidad civil* is the minimum level of third-party car insurance and covers only third-party claims for injury and damage.

- *Responsabilidad civil, incendio y robo* is classically a third-party, fire and theft policy which covers a vehicle for fire, natural hazards, theft, broken windscreen and some legal costs. Theft or damage to contents is not usually included.

- *Todo riesgo* is a fully comprehensive insurance covering all damage to a vehicle.

Procedures following an accident are the same in Spain as the UK, but things do take longer, which is unfortunate when a damaged car needs to be repaired quickly. With small accidents drivers can settle the matter themselves and if need be inform their insurance companies. In larger accidents the police will appear, taking details with a possible view to charging someone.

It makes sense to contact an insurer quickly in the event of an accident. They will advise on the claim process. In the event of a car being stolen, report it to the police immediately and claim from the insurance company, submitting a copy of the *denuncia*. Equally, if you are determined to make a charge against the other driver, start with a *denuncia* and then ask the insurers for advice.

Some people living in a twilight zone of 'long-stay non-residents' may wish to retain their foreign car in Spain. The car is legally required to be insured in the country of registration, e.g. the UK, but this can be difficult if it has never returned for its MOT. There are ways round this as Spanish branches of UK insurance companies insure a car using a Spanish *ITV* test. While this may satisfy an insurance company that a vehicle is in sound operating condition, it has no other legal force as it remains illegal in both the UK and Spain because it has no MOT. In order to maintain this 'tourist charade' a driver will also need to drive on a UK licence and ignore the six-month rule for imported vehicles.

CAR RENTAL

With 50 million tourists per year Spain has a large, competitive rental market. For a small car look to pay around 200€ per week in summer and 150€ in winter. Most companies have special low rates for weekend rentals and for periods longer than 14 days. Rates between major international companies vary little.

Ensure that a car has air conditioning and check the position on collision damage waiver (*cobertura de danos por colision*), theft cover (*cobertura contra robo*), personal accident insurance (*asistencia por lesiones personales*), and the number of additional drivers.

Drivers must be at least 22 years old and a number of companies have an upper age limit of 65. UK drivers must produce a valid licence (a copy is not acceptable) and non-EU drivers an international driving licence.

MOTOR SCOOTERS

Forty-nine cc motor scooters are a radical alternative to a motor car, particularly for nipping through city traffic. There is absolutely no fuss getting one! A Spanish child of 14 years can get one. For the more mature driver all that is required is a driving licence – any type will do – and about 2,500€ to buy the machine.

Insurance is expensive, from 325€ per year because of the high risk involved, and don't expect to obtain cover for theft as these convenient little machines are popular with robbers. (Registration plates are required for a scooter with an engine capacity below 50cc.) Scooters, or mopeds as they are sometimes called, are not permitted on motorways and riders must use cycle paths where provided. At 16 it is possible to ride a light motorcycle (*motocicleta*) with an engine capacity of up to 125cc and at age 18 a motorcycle over 125cc, for which a motorcycle licence (*licencia de conduccion de ciclomotores*) is required.

MOTORING OFFENCES

Parking fines

No one pays a parking fine. It is a relatively small charge. Refusing to pay results in municipality costs which are too high to pursue the issue through a court. People know this and take advantage of the situation. Responsible residents are allowed 15 days to pay or formally protest a fine. A fine may be increased if not paid within a prescribed period.

So what are local town halls doing to overcome the problems of illegal parking, particularly double parking, assuming they are themselves blameless with adequate parking lots provided? Answers below.

- Charge high parking fines of 75€ as a major deterrent.

- Charge very high parking fines for repeated offenders.

- Tow a car away with a recovery fee of around 75€ in addition to a parking fine.

- Wheel clamp.

A garage or entrance permitting access for a vehicle to a house or building at all times is subject to an annual tax. The entrance must display the sign *vado permanente*. If anyone obstructs the entrance the owner has the right to have the vehicle legally towed away.

Random document checks

The police often set up check points stopping motorists randomly to check their identification and car papers. A passport or *residencia*, a driving licence, vehicle registration papers (*permiso de circulacion*) and insurance certificate should be kept with the car. Since this is impracticable, it is better to make a copy of the papers and keep them in the glove box. In law it is no longer necessary to carry originals.

Multas

On-the-spot fines (*multas*) of up to 302€ can be imposed on non-residents for a range of minor traffic offences such as speeding, not being in possession of car papers or a copy of them, and not wearing a seat belt. The list is not exclusive. The police may escort a non-resident to a bank or location where the money can be obtained. A resident is not required to pay on the spot fines, only non-residents who are so untrustworthy they can flee the country without paying.

Classification of offences

Motoring offences are classified as minor (*leve*), serious (*grave*) and very serious (*muy grave*).

- Minor offences which carry fines of up to 91€ include parking violations and many other offences.

- Serious offences which carry fines from 91€ to 301€ with a possible three-month licence suspension include speeding at less than 50 per cent over the limit and other offences.

- Very serious offences that carry fines from 302€ to 602€, an automatic three-month licence suspension and a possible period in jail, include driving under the influence of alcohol or drugs, refusing to take a breathalyser test, exceeding the speed limit by 50 per cent or at least 30km/h, reckless driving and other offences.

Not all offences or fines fit within the convenient classification above. Fines for offences such as driving without a licence, without a number plate, or driving an unregistered or improperly registered vehicle, or improper use of a mobile phone, range up to 1,503€.

People who commit three serious offences within a two-year period must undergo a refresher course or take a driving test to avoid losing their licence. People who commit three very serious offences within a two-year period automatically lose their licence, although they are offered the possibility of taking a special driving course in which case the licence is suspended for only three months.

Payment and appeal

Residents and non-residents who pay promptly receive a 30 per cent discount if they pay a fine within ten days. The 30 per cent discount does not apply to serious or very serious offences. A *boletin de denuncia* is issued specifying the offence and fine. It is possible to appeal against this and there are instructions on the back of the *boletin de denuncia* explaining how. A written appeal must be made within ten days of an offence to the provincial traffic department in the province where the offence took place. The police will decide whether to uphold an appeal but there is no further appeal against their decision.

FURTHER INFORMATION

Real Automovil Club de Espana. Tel: 902 120 441 or www.race.es

Michelin online map service www.viamichelin.com

16

Birth, Marriage, Divorce and Death

INTRODUCTION

Registering a birth, arranging a marriage or filing for a divorce are similar in Spain to most European countries. There are some complications with dual nationality but this too is found in most countries.

For UK nationals, marriage is simpler in Gibraltar than in a Spanish church or in a local civic office.

Death is dealt with quickly, sympathetically and efficiently, mindful of the requirements of burial and the stress involved for loved ones.

BIRTH

Registration of a birth must be made within eight days at the *Registro Civil* (Spanish civil registry where births, marriages and deaths are recorded) in the town where the birth takes place. Registration applies to everyone irrespective of nationality or residential status. If a child is born in Spain it must be registered in Spain. The birth is certified in the normal way by a doctor, or an official of the hospital, or a registered midwife. It includes the hour, date and place of birth, the child's first and last names, the full names of both parents and identification of the person completing the certificate.

There are two forms of birth certificate (*inscripcion de nacimiento*):

- a short certificate called a *Certificacion Extracto* which gives the birth date, the names of the child and parents and is sufficient for most legal purposes;

- a full certificate called a *Certificacion Literal* containing all details of the birth.

Unusually a birth certificate must state whether a child is legitimate or illegitimate (an illegitimate child is born less than 180 days after its parents' marriage or within 300 days of a divorce, annulment of a marriage or death of a father).

A UK citizen is required to report a birth to the British Consulate in Spain which will require a full certificate before issuing a birth certificate for their own country. Parents' passports, full birth certificates, marriage certificate (not the *Libro de Famila*) and any divorce decree will also be required to complete the paperwork. The Consulate then issues a certificate of the birth of a citizen abroad.

Birth registration by parents of a child for British citizenship, who are not married, is more complex. A child is entitled to British citizenship if the mother was born in the United Kingdom. There is no provision at the British Consulate for the registration of births of children where only the father is British and the parents are not married. However, British born fathers are able to register their children who are born abroad via the Home Office. Where parents are not married, it is necessary for both of them to make a paternity declaration if the father's details are to be shown on the birth certificate.

A child born to foreign parents in Spain is not Spanish even if its parents are residents of Spain at the time, but should the child, at age 18, choose to apply for Spanish citizenship it will be granted, particularly if he or she has been living in Spain for most of the time. If one of the child's parents is Spanish the child is entitled to Spanish nationality. A child born out of wedlock, where the nationality of the father is not disclosed, is also entitled to Spanish nationality, regardless of the nationality of the mother.

Abortion

Abortion is legal and tolerated by the Catholic Church. Spain does not have abortion on demand. It is available during the first 12 weeks of pregnancy in certain circumstances, e.g. when a pregnancy threatens the mother's life, the foetus is severely deformed or the pregnancy was the result of rape. Recent attempts to liberalise this law have met with failure.

MARRIAGE

Civil and religious marriages (Roman Catholic, Protestant, Jewish and Muslim) can be celebrated in Spain for people over 18 years of age. Spanish law permits foreigners to marry in Spain but it is necessary for one of the couple to have been legally resident in Spain for at least two years. An application for marriage in Spain will usually involve lengthy and time-consuming paperwork, and applicants should therefore allow enough time before the intended date of marriage for the application to be processed.

Spanish civil marriages

Applications for civil marriages must be made to the civil registry or district court in the place where the marriage is to be celebrated. If one of the parties is resident in the UK, and intends to come to Spain shortly before the ceremony, they should contact the Spanish Consulate for information as it may be possible to start the application process there. If proof of UK residence is necessary, a letter can be obtained from the local electoral registration office, stating that the applicant is on an electoral register for that year. If the applicant who is resident in the UK is required to produce a Certificate of No Impediment, the notice of marriage can be displayed in their local town hall and a registrar can issue the certificate. This will then have to be exchanged for the Spanish equivalent at the nearest British Consulate in Spain. The marriage can be held at a court building, the Spanish Civil Registry office, or very fashionably at a town hall with a judge or mayor presiding.

Spanish religious marriages

The requirements for religious marriages vary according to the denomination and the area in which an applicant lives. Spain is a predominately Catholic country, so to be married in a Roman Catholic Church normal practice applies where at least one partner must be a Catholic and a divorcee is not permitted to marry in a church if the previous marriage was solemnised there. Religious marriages are recognised as legal under Spanish law, but to obtain an official marriage certificate, and for it to be legal under UK law, the marriage must subsequently be registered with the local civil authorities. Therefore it is important to confirm an officiator at the marriage is licensed to marry and to establish arrangements for civil registration.

Spanish marriages ... the forms!

The documents required will vary for civil and religious marriages, and in different areas of Spain. The following is a list of some of the documents that may be required.

- An original full birth certificate, accompanied by a sworn translation into Spanish and authenticated by the Spanish Foreign Ministry, with the Hague Apostille affixed.

- A Certificate of Residence (*Certificado de Empadronamiento*), proving residence in Spain of at least two years which is available from the local town hall.

- A marriage and divorce/annulment/death certificate, if either applicant has been married previously.

- A statement of proof that both parties are free to marry, which can take various forms, such as a letter from both sets of parents, or a Consular Certificate of No Impediment to marriage. This can only be issued after a notice of intention to marry is published on a Consular notice board for a clear 21 days. The notice must be sworn by an applicant, and can only be accepted if the applicant declares that they have been residing for a twenty-one day period in the area where the notice is displayed.

- A consular registration certificate.

- A residence card or passport.

- A baptismal certificate, for Catholic marriages.

- An application form, for civil marriages, available from the civil registry.

Documents that are in English will usually need to have a sworn translation attached. In some cases they may need to bear the Hague Apostille which is available from the Foreign and Commonwealth Office in London.

Marrying a Spaniard does not make a foreigner automatically a Spaniard. A husband or wife will have to apply for Spanish nationality which will normally be granted.

Gibraltar

Many British people often find it easier to get married in Gibraltar, where the ceremony takes place in a registry office in front of two witnesses. The colony has special regulations, which allow 'quickie marriages' by the Governors' Special Licence for non-residents. Proof of not being married to someone else, swearing an affidavit at the Registry Office, paying about 100€ results in the official papers being available in two days. Address: Civil Status and Registration Office, Marriage Registry, 277 Main Street, Gibraltar. Tel: 9767 72289/78303 from Spain.

Common law relationships

A couple may live together for many years as man and wife and have children together, but this establishes no legal rights for either the man or the woman. If a man dies, the woman has no claim to inherit any share of his assets. Children are regarded as being born to a single mother, taking her name and nationality. The inheritance tax paid by a mother or children in the event of the father's death is higher than that of a married couple.

Parejas de Hecho is a term used to describe unmarried partners of the same or opposite sex living together as a family who have committed themselves to a lasting relationship at a private ceremony. Some provinces have established voluntary registration but this list confers no additional legal rights except in the *comunidads* of Madrid and Andalusia. Same sex couples can now legally marry.

Libro de Familia

A 'family book' (*Libro de Familia*) is the official registration of husband, wife and their children which Spaniards are presented with when they come of age, when they marry and when they die. The term *Libro de Familia* is used in tax returns to identify changes in family members.

Spanish names are important. They are designated at birth and marriage. A mother's maiden name is added to the end of a full name at birth, women do not change their name when they marry, and the prefix of Don or Dona is introduced at the start of a name in formal documents. It is also customary to address people as Senor, Senora or Senorita.

Example

Senor Don John Frederick Smith King is simply Mr John Smith with a middle name Frederick and a mother's maiden name King. He is married to Senora Dona Maria Dolores Sanchez Vicario. Conchita Smith Sanchez is their daughter Conchita.

DIVORCE

Internationally accepted grounds for divorce apply – namely adultery, desertion, cruelty, alcohol or drug addiction and mental problems, but the simplest procedure is divorce by mutual consent which is carried out by a *notario* with documents submitted by an *abagodo*. At the same time the couple is required to settle their financial arrangements, child support and visiting rights of children. Having lived apart for one year there is another brief hearing and if nothing has changed, the divorce is granted. Where the separation is not by mutual consent, the period of legal separation is five years before a divorce is granted.

Foreigners, both or singularly, who have been married in another country for at least one year and where at least one is now resident in Spain, can petition in Spain for a divorce which will be recognised in their home country.

It is wise to consult an *abagodo* when seeking a divorce.

DEATH

The death of a relative or friend is always distressing but if it happens abroad the distress can be made worse by practical problems. Spanish procedures differ significantly to those in the UK. In the event of death, a certificate must be prepared and signed by the doctor who attended the death and legally certified by a judge. A death, like a birth, must be registered at the *registro civil* of the district where it took place. If the deceased was a foreigner, a passport or *residencia* card is required. An international death certificate will then be issued. When a person dies several copies of the death certificate will be provided for banks and execution of a will.

Standard procedure

Except in remote rural areas, Spanish undertakers are modern, well-equipped organisations accustomed to working with foreigners. Most have at least one English-speaking staff member. Following the death of a British national in Spain, the next of kin, or a formally appointed representative, must decide whether to repatriate the deceased to the UK, or carry out a local burial or cremation. Under a strict interpretation of Spanish law, a deceased person must be buried after 24 hours and before 72 hours of death. However, in the case of foreign nationals the authorities will normally allow as much time as necessary, although this should not be longer than a few days.

Funeral directors are aware that family members are distraught when someone has died. They provide a full service, including all paperwork, so only one telephone call is necessary to set the process in motion. If no doctor has yet pronounced the person dead, they will locate a doctor to do so and they will inform the Spanish judge who officially issues the death certificate. The funeral director takes the passport data of the deceased and arranges for the official certificates to be delivered to a family.

The British Consulate in Spain can supply additional advice together with a list of international undertakers.

Repatriation

If the deceased was covered by travel insurance, the insurance company will normally have a standing agreement with an international funeral director in Britain to arrange repatriation. If the deceased is not covered by insurance the next of kin will need to appoint an undertaker in Spain or an international funeral director themselves. Spanish undertakers have links with international undertakers in the UK and they normally work well together to ensure that all necessary requirements are met. Local undertakers in Spain are equipped to carry out repatriation procedures and can provide the special caskets required for the international carriage of human remains. A civil registry death certificate, plus the doctor's death certificate (indicating cause of death), a certificate of embalming, and a certificate giving permission to transfer the remains to the UK are required to ship a body. This will be arranged by the Spanish undertaker. The British Consulate can provide covering certificates for British Customs.

Local burial

If the next of kin choose to proceed with a local burial, they will need to instruct a local funeral director. The deceased will probably need to be registered as an inhabitant of the municipality in order to be buried in the local cemetery so a *certificado de empadronamiento* is necessary. Although cemeteries in Spain are mostly Catholic, a person of any creed can be buried there. In most Spanish cemeteries, internment is above ground and bodies are placed in niches set into walls, which are rented for only five years. Unless specifically purchased in perpetuity after the rental period has expired, bodies are interred in a common burial ground within the consecrated cemetery grounds.

Local cremation

Cremation (known as *incineracion*) is now widely accepted in Spain and except in rural areas; there are modern, well equipped, crematoria. Family members are not allowed to attend the cremation itself. They may hold a religious service before the cremation, with the body present, or after it, with the urn. If next of kin choose local cremation and wish to take the ashes back to the UK themselves, they can do so with minimal bureaucracy. If this is not possible, local undertakers will be able to arrange the necessary paperwork and transportation. There is no restriction on movement of ashes within the EU.

Inquests

If the circumstances of death were not unusual, registration of the death is completed and the body will be released for repatriation or burial within a few hours. However, if an examining magistrate is not satisfied after a preliminary examination of the facts, an autopsy may be required. Further investigations and interviews with witnesses may also be called for before a decision is made about the cause of death. In cases of sudden or unexpected death, whether by accident or misadventure, or where a person dies unattended, the examining magistrate will prepare a report of their findings and the body will be released for burial. The magistrate's report will be retained by the court and may only be released to the legal representative of the next of kin. However, if death was caused by a criminal act, the police will be ordered to conduct a full investigation. The state prosecutor will then decide whether to prosecute. This can delay the release of the body for burial.

Autopsies

Autopsies are carried out by court-appointed forensic doctors. During an autopsy organs can be removed for testing, including toxicological studies, at the discretion of the doctor, without consent of the next of kin. Next of kin are not informed about the removal of any organs. The deceased's body can be buried or cremated in Spain or returned to the UK before tests on removed organs are completed. Any organs removed are retained for the duration of the tests, and are then put in storage for at least one month before being destroyed. The next of kin can seek a court order requiring the eventual return of these organs. If the deceased's body has been repatriated, the next of kin should contact their local coroner in the UK in order to request the return of any organs removed.

Organs for research or transplants must have approval in the will of the deceased or from the next of kin. A simple telephone call to the appropriate university is all that is required for the body to be removed.

UK coroners

When a body is repatriated to England or Wales, a coroner will hold an inquest only if the death was violent or unnatural, or if the death was sudden and the cause unknown. Consequently coroners may order a post-mortem as part of the inquest. Coroners can request copies of post-mortem and police reports from the Spanish authorities. However, these will only be provided once any judicial proceedings are completed. In some instances this can take many months. In Scotland, the Scottish Executive is the responsible authority. However, they are not obliged to hold an inquest into the cause of death. Coroners in Northern Ireland are also not obliged to hold an inquest into the cause of death. However, the next of kin can apply for a judicial review if no inquest is held.

Release of information

Access to information concerning a death, other than post-mortem and police reports, is restricted. The Spanish authorities will not provide this information direct to next of kin, or to third parties including the British Consulate. Requests for this information should be made through a legal representative. The release of any information can take many months and the documents will be in Spanish.

Consular death registration

There is no obligation for the death overseas of a British national to be registered with the British Consulate. However, there are the advantages that a British form of death certificate is then available, and that a record of the death is afterwards held at the General Register Office in the UK.

FURTHER INFORMATION

British Embassy in Madrid or any British Consulate Office in Spain.

Spanish Embassy in London or any Spanish Consulate Office in London, Edinburgh or Manchester.

17
Wills and Inheritance Tax

INTRODUCTION

Two definitions!

* A will (*testamento*) is a legal declaration of how a person wishes their possessions to be distributed after death.

* To inherit is to receive a property, money, or title from a parent, ancestor or another person by legal succession.

An inheritance is a mirror of a will. Linked to both is taxation of an inheritance.

Readers of this book will probably be a couple either married or unmarried, resident or non-resident in Spain. They may also be a single person resident or non-resident. They will probably be British (Scottish, Northern Ireland, Wales and England) at birth, with a property and some assets in Spain. So this chapter considers the testator law of both the UK and Spain and how it would affect readers, together with Spanish inheritance tax and some legitimate methods of tax avoidance.

MAKING A WILL

Which country?

A person with British nationality at birth will find that Spanish authorities permit an estate to be bequeathed to whoever they choose, so long as this is allowed by their own national law. However a Spanish estate is subject to Spanish inheritance tax. Anyone with assets in Spain should make a Spanish will disposing of their Spanish assets in order to avoid time-consuming and expensive legal problems for heirs. A separate will should be made for disposing of assets located in the UK. Make sure a UK will states clearly it disposes only of assets in that country and make sure a Spanish will disposes only of assets in Spain.

Spanish inheritance law applies theoretically to British citizens with a property in Spain. Both Spain and the UK have laws which state that the disposal of property will be governed by the law of the country in which the property is located. However, a Spanish Certificate of Law ensures that when a foreign property owner dies, the disposal of any assets in Spain will be governed by their own national law, not Spanish law. Confusing and contradictory!

In practice the Spanish authorities do not ask if a testator is an official resident or not. They accept as valid a Spanish will disposing of Spanish property according to the law of another country. The only requirement by Spanish authorities is payment to Spain of inheritance tax on property or assets located in Spain.

UK laws

UK law (England, Wales and Northern Ireland) permits free disposal of an estate. Scottish law requires that some portion of the estate be left to surviving children. In other words an estate in whole or part can be left to anyone including the dogs' home. Compare this to the restrictive law of Spain which is known as the law of compulsory heirs (*herederos forzosos*).

Spanish laws

Spanish inheritance laws restrict the testator's freedom to leave their property to anyone. Spanish law requires a testator to divide the estate into three equal parts.

One-third must be left to the children in equal parts. Another third must also be left to the children, but the testator may decide how to divide it with the surviving spouse having a life interest in this part. A life interest is a controlling interest as the child who inherits it cannot dispose of it freely until their surviving parent dies. The final third of the estate can be willed to anyone.

This is not quite as brutal for the surviving spouse as it may seem initially, as he or she keeps all assets acquired before the marriage, half of the assets acquired during marriage, and all inheritances which have come directly to the spouse. In effect this means that half of the assets do not really form part of the deceased person's estate. Half the property continues to belong to the surviving spouse.

So what is a possible outcome of all this? Take a married Spanish couple with two children. One of the parents dies and they own a property which if sold is worth 150,000€.

The spouse retains 75,000€ acquired during marriage. The value of the estate is the other half which is obviously 75,000€.

Each child is allocated half of one-third of 75,000€, in this case 12.500€ each.

Let us say the eldest son retains one-third, in this case 25,000€ with a controlling interest, called an *usofructo*, held by the spouse.

Probably the final third of 25,000€ is left to the spouse. The spouse's total holding is now effectively 100,000€ with a controlling interest in a further 25,000€, in total 83 per cent.

Spanish inheritance laws are inflexible. They aim to preserve the family unit by ensuring a property is handed down from generation to generation. In this example the property now has three owners and all three have to agree before it can be sold. An extremely unlikely scenario! More likely would be one child buying out the other child's share upon the death of the other parent.

Contesting a Spanish will

The law of both the UK and Spain states that the inheritance laws of the country will apply where the property or asset is situated. But Spain chooses not to apply this provided inheritance tax is paid to them. So what happens when a British citizen leaves a Spanish property to a dogs' home, which is perfectly possible under English law, but children contest the will, stating they are entitled to two-thirds of the asset under Spanish law? After all, the Spanish authorities are choosing not to apply their own laws. Answer – the children would win the case. It is better to eliminate grounds for contesting a will if a controversial one is to be written.

Dying intestate

If a UK resident or non-resident dies intestate, the estate in Spain will be distributed according to Spanish laws. If a British resident or non-resident dies with only an all embracing will for all assets this will still be applied, but there will be some considerable delay and cost before it can be finalised. Specialist legal assistance is necessary in both countries. This is a strong argument for making a Spanish will.

How to make a will for Spanish assets

Making a Spanish will for Spanish assets according to the inheritance laws of the UK is quite straightforward provided the *abagodo* and notary understand they are not rubber-stamping Spanish succession laws. A husband and wife who own half the property as stated in an *escritura* are required to make separate wills as they own their property share separately. A will is made out by an *abagodo*, authorised by the *notario* and signed in their presence by witnesses. It is called a *testamento abierto*. The notary keeps the original with the testor receiving an authorised copy. Notification is made to a central registry in Madrid, called the *Registro Central de Ultima Voluntad*. Wills are filed there under a reference number and name of the notary.

INHERITANCE TAX

Domicile

There are many issues that can affect a liability to inheritance tax, including the country of domicile.

Under UK law it is necessary to have a country of domicile for tax purposes. This will usually be the place with which a person has the closest connection – normally the country of birth rather than the place in which they are currently living.

If you are not intending to return to live in Britain, it may be possible to establish an alternative domicile by taking steps to show that a new home abroad is permanent. You would then be classed as UK non-domiciled which can be extremely advantageous for tax purposes in an obscure tax haven, but definitely not in Spain.

So to put it simply, a UK citizen, with a UK passport, resident or non-resident in Spain is still domiciled in the UK unless steps are taken to change this. Although this assumption is made for the balance of this chapter it is to some extent irrelevant, for inheritance tax for Spanish assets is paid to Spain.

Guidelines

Inheritance tax is regarded by many as the cruelest of taxes. Having spent a lifetime paying income tax yet another lump of assets amassed over the years will be claimed back by the tax authorities. With careful planning people need pay little or nothing in inheritance tax. It was once described as a 'voluntary levy paid by those who distrust their heirs more than they dislike the *Hacienda*'.

On death, the surviving spouse or dependants have six months to inform the authorities and pay any inheritance tax. If this is not done, with the property remaining in the deceased's name, it cannot be sold. There are also penalties for the non-payment of Spanish inheritance tax on time.

Spanish inheritance tax is payable when an inheritor is a resident of Spain, or the asset inherited is property in Spain. Spanish inheritance tax is not payable if the asset is outside Spain and the recipient is not a resident in Spain.

Inheritance tax is the liability of each beneficiary and not of the deceased's estate. Surprisingly the actual tax payable is based on four factors:

- the amount bequeathed;

- tax exemptions and allowances;

- the relationship of the recipient to the deceased;

- wealth of the recipient.

There is no exemption between a husband and wife where each holds joint ownership of a property. In many countries a property can be held in joint names. If one person dies the property passes automatically to the other person. This is not the case in Spain where each person holds an equal share. Upon the death of one person, the other is subject to inheritance tax when inheriting the other half.

Spanish inheritance taxation law does not recognise a common law spouse. The relationship has no legal standing. They have no inheritance tax exemptions. They are also taxed at a premium rate and treated as non-relatives.

Inheritance tax structure mirrors the Spanish law of 'compulsory heirs' and takes an old-fashioned view of marriage.

Setting a value on the deceased's estate

Property is valued either at market value, a value in the *IBI* statement, the value in the *escritura* or a value set by the *Hacienda*, whichever is greater. Stocks and shares, cars and bank accounts are valued at the date of death. The value of life insurance settlement is dependent on the recipient. Furniture, clothing and personal effects (*ajuar*) are treated as gifts having no value.

Exemptions

The law provides an individual exemption from tax of the first 16,000€ bequeathed where an estate is passed to a spouse, parents, children, brothers and sisters. This exemption applies to each inheritor, not to the total estate. For uncles, cousins and nephews, the exemption is cut by half to 8,000€. For more distant relatives, people not related and common law couples, there is no exemption. Conversely children aged 13 to 21 years of age attract higher exemptions. This applies to residents and non-residents.

Inheritance tax can be significantly reduced where a resident of Spain leaves a principal residence to a spouse, children, or a brother or sister (over 65 years), who has lived with the deceased for two years. All are eligible for a 95 per cent exemption in inherited value up to a maximum of 120,000€. To qualify, the *residencia* must have been held for three years, the property must have been lived in for three years and the inheritors must undertake not to sell the property for ten years. This exemption is only for a home or a family business and does not apply to investments or second homes. Non-resident holiday home owners cannot take advantage of this exemption.

Inheritance tax tables

Taxable amount €	Tax payable €	Tax %
8,000	600	7.5%
16,000	1,300	8.0%
32,000	2,900	9.0%
48,000	4,700	9.8%
64,000	6,800	10.6%
80,000	9,200	11.5%
120,000	15,600	13.0%
160,000	23,000	14.4%
240,000	40,000	16.7%
400,000	80,000	20.0%

Table 1. Extract from inheritance tax tables: basic tax rates.

Tax table 1 is a rounded abbreviated extract from a full table. It is for guidance only. To use this table take the amount inherited, less any allowances highlighted in the previous section, subtract any debts owed by the deceased such as an unpaid mortgage and funeral expenses. This is the taxable amount with corresponding tax payable.

Wealth of inheritor €	Multiplying coefficient		
	A	B	C
0 to 400,000	1.00	1.60	2.00
400,000 to 2,000,000	1.05	1.70	2.10
2,000,000 to 4,000,000	1.10	1.75	2.20
+ 4,000,000	1.20	1.90	2.40

A = children, adopted children, grandchildren, spouses, parents, grandparents

B = cousins, nieces, nephews, distant relatives, descendants and ascendants

C = all others, including unmarried partners

Table 2. Inheritance tax multiplier.

Tax table 2 multiplies tax payable in table 1 by a factor ranging from 1.0 to 2.4 depending on the wealth of the recipient and their relationship to the deceased. In fact table 1 only applies to children, adopted grandchildren, grandchildren, spouses, parents and grandchildren who have a personal wealth less than 400,000€. All other benefactors, including those with high personal wealth and unmarried couples, pay more.

The Spanish inheritance tax system penalises inheritance to non-relations and to the rich. It is designed to maintain a family structure and benefit the poor.

Regional variations

Madrid, Catalonia and Valencia have different inheritance tax rates. Madrid has inheritance laws stating that unmarried couples can take advantage of the lower tax rates applied to married couples providing they are on the local register of unmarried couples.

Andalusia tax authorities have eliminated inheritance tax for individual family inheritors who are official residents of Andalusia and receive less than 125,000€. The 95 per cent allowance also rises to 99.9 per cent. The total value of the estate should not exceed 500,000€ and the wealth of each inheritor should not exceed 400,000€. Registered unmarried and same-sex couples also obtain this exemption.

These regional variations now recognise and come to terms with some of the old fashioned principles of Spanish inheritance tax.

Examples

In order to better understand the computation of inheritance tax, three examples are chosen. They all start with a property valued at 300,000€ held in joint ownership. One person dies and bequeaths the other half of the property to the surviving spouse. They have two children. The examples look at different combinations of resident, non-resident, married and non-married. For the benefit of simplicity the figures are rounded and the location is not one with regional tax variations.

1 Married couple, non-resident – a typical holiday home owner

Value bequeathed	150,000€
Allowance	16,000€ (individual exemption)
Taxable amount	134,000€
Tax payable	18,000€

2 Married couple, resident – a typical ex-pat

Value bequeathed	150,000€
Allowance	136,000€ (120,000€ + 16,000€)
Taxable amount	14,000€
Tax payable	1,300€

3 Unmarried couple, resident

Value bequeathed	150,000€
Allowance	nil
Taxable amount	300,000€ (multiplying coefficient of 2.0)
Tax payable	55,000€

In the first example the total inheritance tax bill would be halved if the property was left in equal parts to the children and surviving spouse. In the third example the tax bill would be 1,300€ if the couple married or lived in Andalusia.

LEGITIMATE METHODS OF AVOIDING SPANISH INHERITANCE TAX

Over the years many methods have been used to lessen the impact of this tax. Some of these have been illegal and led to greater problems and higher taxation at a later date. These methods have included the non-declaration of death, under-declaring the value of assets and using a power of attorney after death. With the introduction of new European tax laws on disclosure these practices will become a thing of the past. No professional advisor will risk high fiscal penalties for the sake of assisting clients in evading taxation.

Trusts

One such method is to create a trust, in which assets pass into the hands of a company, with each family member becoming a shareholder. When one member dies, the shares are transferred to other family members. This attracts little tax. The location of this company may be offshore. Making a trust is best left to experts. It attracts annual charges and therefore is best suited to large financial holdings. The only real alternative to a will is to set up a trust structure during a lifetime. With careful planning this can eradicate delays, administration costs and taxes, as well as giving other benefits. For these reasons the use of trusts can be quite dramatic. A trust is not dissimilar to a will except that assets are transferred to trustees during a lifetime, rather than being transferred to executors on death. The trust deed is comparable to the will.

Life interest

You can transfer the property to a chosen heir while still alive and maintain a *usufructo* over it, retaining a right of use while living. The ownership has formally passed to another person. This legal move, which is viewed by the tax authorities as a gift, still attracts some inheritance tax, albeit at a reduced level, depending on the age of the people involved.

A simpler solution can be achieved by selling the property to a chosen heir. We do know that selling a property can cost around ten per cent of its value so in the previous examples this will be 30,000€. Compare this to the tax bill for an unmarried couple! A life expectancy of five years is however necessary as tax authorities assume – quite correctly – that this it is to avoid tax.

Equity release

Some companies are offering an equity release facility to individuals owning a property in Spain.

However, this should not be confused with schemes offered in the United Kingdom and certain other countries where elderly individuals are to accept a lump sum payment in lieu of the 'sale' of their property, and continue to live in it rent free for the remainder of their lives. After their deaths the beneficiaries have no financial interest in the property as legal title belongs to the lender. This form of arrangement does not exist in Spain.

Most of the equity release schemes in Spain are in effect remortgages. These schemes allow a property owner to take out a mortgage, normally without capital repayments, against the security of his or her property. Provided the borrowed funds are properly reinvested outside of Spain, this is likely to reduce Spanish inheritance tax on death. The loan can be as much as 100 per cent of the property valuation for suitable applicants, and most lenders will agree the loan in most leading currencies, although the interest rate will vary according to the currency chosen. The lender may allow some of the loan monies to be used as so wished, but will require most of it to be invested and offered as further security for the loan. A typical loan is for a five-year period, after which it would have to be renegotiated. The lender may not be obliged to renew and may demand repayment at the end of the original loan period.

To avoid inheritance tax in this way all the normal rules must be followed. For a Spanish tax resident, the mortgage will reduce net assets in Spain. Of course, the loan proceeds must be invested outside Spain, either via a trust for beneficiaries or in a will to non-Spanish residents. If you are not a Spanish tax resident, the mortgage proceeds must be invested outside Spain and should not pass to any Spanish residents on death.

These equity release schemes only aim to reduce Spanish inheritance tax; if you are a UK domicile, upon death these schemes will not reduce any UK inheritance tax liability.

Give it away

This is by far the most generous concession on inheritance. It allows anyone to give away anything they like, including cash, property or works of art, with no tax liability whatsoever. Again there is one condition – the gifting person must remain alive for at least five years after making the transfer.

Investments and UK inheritance tax

Think carefully where investments are located. It may be that investments are better located in an offshore trust so this requires no further consideration as they should be protected by some tax avoidance scheme. It may be that investments can be located in the UK or in Spain in which case they should be allocated to the will of that particular country. It is just a matter of doing some calculations. UK inheritance tax liability does not accrue for the items below, over that the tax rate is 40 per cent:

- anything given to a spouse;

- any gift to a charitable body;

- the value of an estate less than £275,000 (excluding anything given to a spouse);

- anything given more than seven years before death;

- on gifts made before death if they did not, in total, exceed £3,000 in any one tax year.

Equalising a UK estate not exceeding £275,000 in value means it is exempt from UK inheritance tax, so married couples should try to equalise their estates to take full advantage of this exemption. If a husband whose wife is wealthy in her own right leaves his entire estate to her, he would only be adding to the potential charge on her estate upon death. Instead, he should consider leaving all or part of his estate direct to other beneficiaries – his children, for example.

Maintaining a loan

Inheritance tax is only payable after debts have been deducted. If it was possible to have a 100 per cent interest-only mortgage or loan then this is a guarantee of no inheritance tax. This is not possible as a mortgage but is possible as a loan. It is a matter of doing the figures. Some financial advisors are only too pleased to do it! Charges are high.

Holiday home owners

A Spanish holiday home owner will probably have a main residence in the UK which will be subject to the inheritance laws of that country. In fact the decreased worldwide assets will be subject to the laws of the UK even if inheritance tax has already been deducted in Spain for the Spanish property. In this situation any tax paid in Spain can be deducted against a UK tax liability to avoid a double tax charge.

CASE STUDY

Question. I have now moved to Spain, having been recently divorced. I have three children from my previous wife and would like to leave my property in Spain to them. I have made a UK will to that effect but I have been told that I have to leave it to my eldest son, as this is Spanish law. Surely I am allowed to do whatever I want with my property even after my death?

Answer. Spanish Succession Law states that the assets of the deceased must be left to the children, although the testator has the right to dispose freely of one-third of the assets. The children are considered to be forced inheritors and cannot be removed without a court order. However, this does not affect a British national as succession is regulated by UK law. Therefore leave the assets to whoever you wish.

It would be better to draw up a Spanish will, limited to assets in Spain. Having a Spanish will avoids unnecessary expenses after death. Although a UK will can be used in Spain, certain requisites have to be observed as below:

1 The original probate and last will have to be legalised by the Foreigners' Office with an *Apostille* in accordance with The Hague Convention of 5 October 1961.

2 Because these documents are in the English language, they have to be translated into Spanish by an official interpreter authorised by the Spanish Foreigners' Office.

3 An application to the Ministry of Justice has to be submitted requesting a certificate to state that there is no last will and testament recorded therein.

Once these have been taken care of, the formal acceptance of the inheritance can take place but are not necessary if a Spanish will is made out in the first place.

DENNEY

The relationship between Spanish and UK inheritance law was not always so clear. It was not until 1999 that the issue was finally cleared up in a landmark judgment known as the Denney case. The issue was Denney, an Englishman who died domiciled in Spain: does Spanish law or English law govern the succession to his estate?

Anthony Denney lived in Spain for many years. He died in 1990 and his Spanish will made his second wife Celia Mercedes Royde-Smith universal legatee, without prejudice to the rights that the children of his first marriage might have under his national law. The question was – were his children entitled to inherit part of the estate as obligatory heirs under Spanish law? It took nine years to find out the answer.

Anthony Denney's three children by his first marriage challenged the widow's claim to the estate in the Spanish Courts, claiming that under Spanish law part belonged to them. Their grounds were that because English Private International Law refers to the law of Spain and Article 12.2 of the Spanish Civil Code accepted the reference back from English law, therefore Spanish law gave them compulsory rights to a part of the estate. However, Article 12.2 of the Civil Code is ambiguous and there were no judgments from the Supreme Court to provide guidance on how it should be interpreted.

It should have been merely a matter of obtaining a definitive judgment on a point of law, but a major complicating factor proved to be the question of the ownership of Denney's collection of modern art, which had been lent by him to the Dallas Museum of Art in 1970. Shortly after Denney's death the museum was instructed, in letters signed by Anthony Denney and later discovered to be forged, to transfer the loan collection to the Museum of Modern Art in Toulouse. Transport costs and insurance were paid for by the City of Toulouse. In 1993 the City formally accepted the collection as a gift from Denney's widow, even though officials knew that it had not been declared to the Spanish tax authorities and that Denney's children by his first marriage had lodged an inheritance claim in the Spanish courts.

The widow denied that the children had any right to bring their inheritance claim before the Spanish courts and also argued that the case should not be heard without the Mayor of Toulouse being present, because the city, which she claimed was now the owner of the collection, would be affected by the outcome. The Mayor of Toulouse, for his part, announced that the litigation in Spain was a private matter in which neither the city nor the state nor the regional council were in any way involved.

The litigation in the Spanish courts followed three stages:

Stage 1 January 1995: The Spanish Court of First Instance found no evidence to suggest that the collection had ever left the deceased's estate; it rejected the widow's argument that the Mayor of Toulouse owned the collection and declared the Denney children forced heirs under Spanish law.

Stage 2 July 1995: The Provincial Appeal Court overturned the decision of First Instance, without considering the substance of the inheritance claim, on the grounds that the Mayor of Toulouse ought to have been called to the case.

Stage 3 27 May 1999: The Supreme Court in Madrid ruled that there were no reasons why the City of Toulouse should have been called to the case and overturned the judgment of the Provincial Appeal Court. Then, after considering recent developments in Private International Law and the trend towards a more restricted application, it rejected the claim of the Denney children and revoked the Judgment of First Instance. The order of the Provincial Appeal Court, ordering the costs at First Instance and of the appeal to be paid by the Denney children, was overturned. No ruling was made in respect of costs because of the complexities of the legal issues involved and the fact that similar cases had never come before the Supreme Court.

FURTHER INFORMATION

The most frequently asked question from ex-pats concerns wills and inheritance. Little information exists on this subject thus making it fertile ground for financial advisors and *abogados*.

18
Parting Shots

We live well in Spain.

Our income comes from pensions, monies stashed offshore or from gainful earnings either in the UK or Spain.

Either way, we live well in Spain.

We will always meet a fellow who out-fumbles us at the bar. A woman who claims to speak Spanish and will gladly translate for a modest fee. Someone who will pay for something next week with possession today. Apartments with hidden mortgages on them, details of which usually end up in the British press, frightening readers into remaining in the UK.

Yes, we do live well in Spain.

All the imported foods and goodies we might have missed are now easily available – British clothes, French cheeses, Belgian beer and Irish newspapers! Not quite the image of good old Spain – a donkey laden with firewood and a little old lady dressed in black with a water jug on her head. They are now sketches in tourist shops.

But we do live well in Spain. That is until something goes wrong!

Perhaps the tax man has discovered undeclared earnings, some Germans have encroached on neighbouring land, a letter has arrived from an obscure official Spanish source, a builder has gone bankrupt, someone has died with confusion over inheritance tax, or the police have stopped us with too much red wine in our stomachs. What do we do? Are we getting conflicting advice?

Of course it's not our fault, at worst just a bit of bad luck. Ignore it, the problem will go away: *no problema*, as the Spanish say. Perhaps we should read this book again? That's a good idea! Why not, it's a good start.

A quick reminder – this book is not gospel. Gospel comes in about 26 leather-bound volumes taking seven years to understand to an acceptable standard. It is a guideline for some of the most common applications of Spanish law affecting a foreigner spending some time in Spain. Laws and regulations are complex and liable to change. But reading this book again should solve most problems or at least point the way.

In no way does this book forbid you from hot-footing it down to a friendly English speaking *abogado* who will ask for a stack of euros for their advice. Going the slow road, a pure legal route, can have few clear decisions and possibly even fewer clear results. The water is rarely, if ever, clear. Black and white gives way to a hundred shades of gray.

Again in no way does this book forbid you from violating what might be loosely called the rules. Sometimes situations force us to examine what is right and what is wrong. We've all been in situations where doing the right thing was obviously the wrong thing to do, and in situations where doing the wrong thing was obviously right. It may start with something simple, such as putting up a garden shed without planning permission. Or it may end up being something of catastrophic proportions such as physically evicting a tenant who does not pay the rent. That's when the phrases 'the end justifies the means' and 'rules are made to be broken' come in handy.

Only do it, however, if you have all the facts and understand the consequences – for we do live well in Spain … and it would be wrong to spoil that notion through a hasty decision.

Index

If you want to know how … to buy to let in Spain

'Today's Spain is a young vibrant country. No land is so diverse or enjoys such an excellent climate. It has a strong personality, is full of rich traditions and has a totally unique culture. Spain is also Europe's biggest holiday playground, playing home to some 50 million foreign visitors each year who enjoy the delights of traditional family holidays on the Islands or Costas whilst many also explore the deep green pastures and cities of northern Spain, or sample the rural way of life.

'Buy-to-let property owners are not commercial property developers since they wish to enjoy the benefits of their purchase too, but they do recognise the conundrum that a home is bought with the heart, a commercial property with the head and a buy-to-let property for fun and profit.'

Harry King

Buy to Let in Spain
How to invest in Spanish property for fun and profit
Harry King

This inspiring book will help you fulfil your dream of a second home in Spain – and provide a steady income too. Buying a home in Spain is not expensive, but the procedures are very different and author Harry King uses his own experience to help you avoid the traps the unwary can fall into. Whether it is how to find a suitable property, how to deal with the Spanish conveyancing and letting system, or how to find tenants and run your property as a business, it's all explained in plain English.

ISBN 1 85703 890 8

If you want to know how … to buy a property in Spain

'Sitting on the porch, in the evening, holding a glass of wine, watching the sun setting over the sea, soon to be followed by a visit to the local tapas bar for some food and drinks. A holiday home or a retirement home in the sun is a dream, but one that can come true.

'When you're buying your property you'll find the buying procedures are very different. Forget the traditional approach of putting in an "offer", arranging a mortgage and asking your solicitor to sort things out. Prospective buyers must carry out research and ask questions themselves, rather than assuming a solicitor will deal with these matters. Learn about the *Abogado*, the Notary, the *Gestor*, the Contract and the *Escritura*. It will make things so much easier.'

Harry King

Buying a Property in Spain
An insider guide to finding a home in the sun
Harry King

'This easy to read guide takes you through the process of setting up home in Spain.' – *Daily Mirror*

'King has packed a lot into his 200 or so pages, with a particularly strong couple of chapters on the legal system of buying property and all the parties to the transaction, clearly explaining the part played by the *gestor*, for example.' – *Living Spain*

ISBN 1 85703 791 X

If you want to know how … to live and work in Spain

'There is only one-way to be sure of what Spain has to offer: come and see it for yourself. Going to Spain to work, for a long-term stay, or for retirement can be a step into the unknown. But if some simple preparation is undertaken it can be a step into sunshine and happiness.'

Harry King

Going to Live in Spain
A practical guide to enjoying a new lifestyle in the sun
Harry King

'Spain has long been a popular destination. This book covers all aspects of relocating there, throwing up information on living in Spain, from its cultural history to the ins and outs of its current economy, the documentation you'll need, and, of course, the all-important climate.'
– *Daily Mirror*

'… tips on how to get the most out of this vibrant country so that you can enjoy your new life to the full.' – *Sunday Telegraph*

ISBN 1 85703 875 4

If you want to know how … to move to Spain

'Possibly for the first time in years we are really happy. Stress is a distant memory. We do have less disposable income than we had in London, but we don't need it. With just a bit more than the minimum amount of money to cover utility bills, clothes and food we can and do live very well. We reflect often on how wise our decision was to move to Spain.'

Tom Provan

Gone to Spain

How you, too, can realise your dream of living in Spain
Tom Provan

Tom Provan, after a long and successful career in marketing and PR took the decision to leave England and move – lock, stock, barrel and dog – to Spain. In this book you'll learn from his experiences. Some are very positive, some are frustrating and some are very funny. But if you are contemplating making the same move there is valuable information here that will help you decide whether this is the right decision for you.

ISBN 1 85703 928 9

If you want to know how ... to live and work in Spain

'The Spanish way of life offers everything from classical guitar played in ancient castles to a multitude of modern hyper- and super-markets. Spain is different in many unexpected ways from other countries and many facets of lifestyle are described in this book as full answers are given to questions such as: 'What is the greatest danger in Spain?', 'How do the Spanish drive?' and 'How do you stay healthy/wealthy/wise?'

'With full travel details and scores of helpful tips, this book provides vital information for anyone moving to Spain, whether to work for a large company or in a self-employed capacity.'

Robert A.C. Richards

Living and Working in Spain
The complete guide to a successful short- or long-term stay
Robert A.C. Richards

Whether you want to live, work, retire, study or holiday in Spain this informative guide tells you what to expect. Discover the realities of Spanish life, and how to make the most of it. There's advice on where to live, buying property, getting around, spending your money wisely and how the health, employment and education systems work.

ISBN 1 85703 278 0

If you want to know how … to get a job abroad

'Whether you are a school-leaver in search of adventure or a retired executive in search of new challenges – or somewhere in between – you should find most of the answers to your questions on working abroad in this combined handbook and directory. It discusses the implications, surveys the wide range of opportunities and offers advice on how to land the job you want. The advice is backed up with a comprehensive reference section providing thousands of contacts both at home and abroad. To those of you who are encouraged to take the plunge, may I wish you a very happy and successful time working abroad.'

Roger Jones

Getting a Job Abroad
The international jobseekers' directory
Roger Jones

'Don't even think about packing your suitcase until you've read this … excellent source of information. Practical advice on finding the country where you can make the most of your skills.' – *The Guardian*

'Do your research thoroughly. Check out *Getting a Job Abroad.*'
– *Cosmopolitan*

'An excellent addition to any careers library … compact and realistic.'
– *Newscheck*

'… highly informative … lots of hard information and a first class reference section.' – *Outbound Newspapers*

ISBN 1 85703 851 7

If you want to know how ... to retire abroad

'Just because you're retired doesn't mean that you are content to sit back and reminisce about the past. Instead you are determined to live life to the full and fulfil as many of your aspirations as you can. These may well involve spending time in a different – probably warmer – clime for part or even all of the year. This book offers suggestions and advice and also provides a wide range of contacts – from estate agents to embassies, from furniture removers to financial advisers. I hope that this guide will prove indispensable in your decision-making, steering you successfully in the right direction.'

Roger Jones

How to Retire Abroad
Your complete guide to a fresh start in the sun
Roger Jones

'Provides advice and hard facts on finding a location, getting there, and coping once you're there – and even contains advice if you decide you want to come back! Invaluable chapters include 'What You Need to Know Before Proceeding' and 'How Much Will It Cost?' The appendices are packed with useful addresses and phone numbers.' – *Daily Mirror*

'... contains much thought-provoking information for those considering spending their golden years abroad.' – *French Property News*

'The guide is an excellent starting point. It represents a very modest investment when one considers the expensive and/or ghastly mistakes that may ensue if important points are overlooked.' – *Living France*

ISBN 1 85703 976 9

How To Books are available through all good bookshops, or you can order direct from us through Grantham Book Services.

Tel: +44 (0)1476 541080
Fax: +44 (0)1476 541061
Email: orders@gbs.tbs-ltd.co.uk

Or via our website
www.howtobooks.co.uk

To order via any of these methods please quote the title(s) of the book(s) and your credit card number together with its expiry date.

For further information about our books and catalogue, please contact:

How To Books
3 Newtec Place
Magdalen Road
Oxford OX4 1RE

Visit our web site at
www.howtobooks.co.uk

Or you can contact us by email at info@howtobooks.co.uk